Praise for
Blockchain for Business

M000118927

"Much has been written about blockchain in the past few years: what it is and what it is not (at various levels of detail), as well as the technology's long-term strategic value for companies, industries, and economies. However, what we've been missing is a practical, operational, 'how to' set of steps for creating, implementing, and operating a blockchain-based solution. This book aims to fill that gap. It's an invaluable tool for anyone ready to take the plunge and start taking advantage of this remarkable technology.

"Most technologies can be implemented one business at a time. Not so with blockchain. Blockchain is particularly valuable when applied to a collection of companies working closely together as a business ecosystem, such as a supply chain. *Blockchain for Business* goes into great detail about what it takes to organize and manage such an ecosystem, including the technical and business models that in the end drive the decisions about whether to join or not, and the governance necessary for a smooth, efficient operations. It also nicely explains the necessary technical expertise and management roles needed to successfully create and operate blockchain frameworks and applications.

"*Blockchain for Business* is an invaluable tool for anyone ready to take the plunge and start taking advantage of this remarkable technology."

—*Irving Wladawsky-Berger, Research Affiliate, MIT; Columnist, WSJ CIO Journal; VP Emeritus, IBM*

"Jai, Jerry, and Nitin have written the guidebook to address the critical knowledge gap that exists between the hype of blockchain and cryptocurrencies and the pragmatic utilization of blockchain technology for transforming businesses. *Blockchain for Business* leverages their firsthand insights and provides a practical approach for business and technical leaders to leverage a proven methodology to drive successful blockchain projects that deliver trust and transparency for all participants."

—*Marie Wieck, General Manager, IBM Blockchain*

"Understand how to capture the power of the trust machine. This book contains a wealth of resources and tools for those looking to apply blockchain solutions in a business environment. A must-read for enterprise executives."

—*Perianne Boring, Founder and President, Chamber of Digital Commerce*

"Jai, Jerry, and Nitin nailed it! *Blockchain for Business* addresses the critical question business leaders are attempting to answer: How does my business derive real, measurable value from blockchain? This is a practical guidebook for both the business and technology leader to help identify business value from blockchain technology in the form of new growth opportunities, sustainable competitive advantage, time savings, cost reductions, and risk mitigation—turning blockchain into business results!"

—*D. Keith Pigues, CEO and Founder, Luminas Strategy, Coauthor* Winning with Customers: A Playbook for B2B

"*Blockchain for Business* is a must-read for executives looking to define blockchain's potential to transform business processes. Jerry, Jai, and Nitin have comprehensively described the key steps business leaders should take to identify the right scope, select the best technology, and establish an appropriate business model and governance structure."

—*Arvind Krishna, SVP, Hybrid Cloud and Director of IBM Research*

BLOCKCHAIN FOR BUSINESS

Jai Singh Arun

Jerry Cuomo

Nitin Gaur

✦✦Addison-Wesley

Boston • Columbus • New York • San Francisco • Amsterdam • Cape Town
Dubai • London • Madrid • Milan • Munich • Paris • Montreal • Toronto • Delhi • Mexico City
São Paulo • Sydney • Hong Kong • Seoul • Singapore • Taipei • Tokyo

For information about buying this title in bulk quantities, or for special sales opportunities (which may include electronic versions; custom cover designs; and content particular to your business, training goals, marketing focus, or branding interests), please contact our corporate sales department at corpsales@pearsoned.com or (800) 382-3419.

For government sales inquiries, please contact governmentsales@pearsoned.com.

For questions about sales outside the U.S., please contact intlcs@pearson.com.

Visit us on the Web: informit.com/aw

Library of Congress Control Number: 2018968178

Copyright © 2019 Pearson Education, Inc.

ISBN-13: 978-0-13-558135-3
ISBN-10: 0-13-558135-4

1   19

Dedicated to

My mom and dad, Saroopi Devi and Phusiya Ram, who gave me existence
in this world; my siblings, who encourage me with admiration; my darling
Varshal, who strengthens my soul with love and inspires me; my daughter
Saachi and son Yogya, who enlighten me with joy every day.

And in memory of my loving brother Mr. Omprakash Arun (1968–2013);
my angel sister Ms. Babita Arun (1988–2016); and my respected father-in-law
Mr. Chandrahas Mayekar (1943–2016).
—Jai Singh Arun

My darling Steph. Not since Lennon and McCartney has there been a
more prolific pair of composers like the two of us.
—Gennaro Cuomo

My parents, for their unconditional love; my spouse Ritu, for her unconditional
support; and my son Neil, who inspires me every day.
—Nitin Gaur

CONTENTS

Foreword   xii
Preface   xvii
Acknowledgments   xxiii
About the Authors   xxvii

Chapter 1   Introduction to Blockchain   1
              Blockchain Beliefs   2
              Enterprise Blockchain   3
              Why Blockchain Matters   4
              The Trailblazers   5
                  Founders   6
                  Scope: Dream Large and Act Incrementally   6
                  Motivation: Driving Momentum within the Ecosystem   7
                  Governance: The Total Is Greater Than the Sum of the Parts   8
              Blockchain for Good   9
                  Reducing Foodborne Illnesses   9
                  Eliminating Big Data Breaches   10
                  Preventing Counterfeiting   11
              Blockchain Questions from Business and Technology Leaders   12

Does Blockchain Apply to My Industry and Business Objectives?   13

How Does Blockchain Drive Top-Line Growth and Competitive
    Advantage for My Business?   14

What Value-Added Business Models Does Blockchain Present?   14

How Does Blockchain Network Governance and Design Work?   15

Do I Need a Dedicated Blockchain Development Team?   15

What Is the Cost of Implementing Blockchain?   15

Other Questions   16

Chapter Summary   16

References   17

Chapter 2   Opportunities and Challenges   19

Disruptive Elements   20

Transparency   21

Immutability   21

Security   22

Consensus   23

Smart Contracts   24

Opportunities   25

Transformative Power of Blockchain   25

Transformative Opportunities   29

Challenges   40

Scope   41

Motivation   42

Governance   43

Technology   45

Chapter Summary   47

References   47

Chapter 3   Understanding the Technology Landscape   49

Blockchain: A Technical Perspective   50

The Four Building Blocks   50

Why Blockchain?   53

Blockchain as a Consumable Technology   54

Blockchain for Enterprises   56

Enterprise View of Blockchain: Technology and Business Domain   57

Litmus Tests to Justify the Application of Blockchain
Technology   61

Technology, Business, and Regulatory Considerations for
Blockchain   63

Essential Maturity Imperatives for Enterprise Blockchain   66

Token Revolution   68

Asset Tokenization: Essential to Powering the Next-Generation
Digital "Instance" Economy   68

Introduction to Tokenization: Understanding the Token
Revolution   69

Various Industry Definitions   72

Token Valuation Models and the Instance Economy   73

Understanding Digital Asset (Token) Fungibility: Opportunities and
Challenges Related to Token Valuation and Blockchain Ecosystems 75

Defining Fungibility   76

Considerations for Meaningful and Sustainable Blockchain-Powered
Business Networks   79

Enterprise Integration: Coexisting with Existing Systems
of Record   82

Blockchain Network Extensibility   83

Blockchain Project Sustainability   84

Chapter Summary   85

References   86

Chapter 4   Business of Business Models   87

Path to Blockchain Enterprise Adoption: A Prescriptive Approach 87

1. Identify an Appropriate Use Case   89

2. Devise a Business Blueprint: Distilling an Existing
Business Process   90

3. Map the Business Blueprint to Technology Tenets: Devising a
Technology Blueprint   91

4. Ensure Enterprise Integration with (Legacy) Enterprise Systems 92

Business Modeling and Design   92

Business Model Considerations   94

Chapter Summary   104

FOREWORD

I'm delighted to provide some context for this enormously thoughtful and eminently practical book, *Blockchain for Business*.

When Alex Tapscott and I wrote the first edition of *Blockchain Revolution* in 2016, we characterized blockchain as a platform for conducting transactions of value. We explained that for nearly four decades, we had the Internet of information. It vastly improved the flow of data within and among firms and people, but it didn't transform the deep architecture of the firm. That's because the Internet was designed to move information from person to person. It wasn't designed to solve what cryptographer David Chaum called the "double-spend problem," the ability to spend a single digital dollar in two places online.[1]

Now for the first time ever we have a native digital medium for value, through which we can transfer any asset—from money and music to votes and intellectual property—peer to peer in a secure and private way. Trust

---

1. David Chaum. "Blind Signatures for Untraceable Payments." *Advances in Cryptology: Proceedings of Crypto 82* (January 1982): 199–203.

is achieved not necessarily by intermediaries like banks or governments, but by cryptography, collaboration, and clever code.

Based on the success of the book, Alex and I founded the Blockchain Research Institute (BRI), a think tank dedicated to investigating blockchain use cases and the leadership required to drive experimentation and change in an organization. Our membership has grown to include global corporations, governments, nonprofit organizations, and members of the blockchain start-up community.

IBM's CEO, Ginni Rometty, recognized the transformative potential of blockchain technology early on, and IBM became a founding member of the BRI. Gennaro "Jerry" Cuomo, co-author of this book, participated in the opening panel of the BRI's first all-member summit in the fall of 2017. His contributions were invaluable to the executives in attendance. Since then, we've expanded the program to nearly 100 projects across 10 industry vertical groups and nine C-suite roles in both the public and private sectors. IBM has been an active member, open to sharing what its teams have learned in their collaborations with Walmart and the Brooklyn Roasting Company on food traceability, with Maersk on digitizing global shipping, and with Unilever on tracking digital ad buying.[2]

The crucible of common experience leads to similar thinking. That's probably why these themes of Jai Singh Arun, Jerry Cuomo, and Nitin Gaur's book, *Blockchain for Business*, resonate so much with our own— and in my view, are spot on.

---

2. Reshma Kamath. "Food Traceability on Blockchain: Walmart's Pork and Mango Pilots with IBM." *Journal of the British Blockchain Association* (June 12, 2018). jbba.scholasticahq.com/article/3712-food-traceability-on-blockchain-walmart-s-pork-and-mango-pilots-with-ibm; IBM Corporation and Brooklyn Roasting Company. "Transparency from Farm to Cup." *The Blockchain Bean*, May 1, 2017. www.ibm.com/thought-leadership/blockchainbean; Larry Dignan. "Unilever Aims to Force More Digital Ad Transparency, Plots Blockchain Pilot with IBM." *ZDNet*, February 12, 2018. www.zdnet.com/article/unilever-aims-to-force-more-digital-ad-transparency-plots-blockchain-pilot-with-ibm; Nicky Morris. "Maersk/IBM Complete Supply Chain Blockchain Pilot." *Ledger Insights*, August 9, 2018. www.ledgerinsights.com/maersk-ibm-supply-chain-blockchain-pilot-tradelens.

Digital identity. Jai, Jerry, and Nitin highlight the role of digital identity throughout *Blockchain for Business*. Indeed, Jai is a thought leader in this area, the co-author of one of IBM's important works, "Trust Me: Digital Identity on Blockchain."[3] This is a big deal, and it was a big idea of the paperback edition of *Blockchain Revolution*. Alex and I underscored the need for *self-sovereign identities*, using blockchain as a means of bootstrapping our identities and enforcing them in any context without a third party. We reported on the work of the Decentralized Identity Foundation (DIF), a consortium of which IBM is a member. DIF was formed to combine "decentralized identities, blockchain IDs, and zero-trust data stores that are universally discoverable."[4] Its working groups are focusing on three big areas—identifiers and discovery, storage and computation of data, and attestation and reputation—with an eye toward developing use cases and standards.[5] IBM has contributed a lot to these endeavors, working with ATB Financial, Evernym, the Sovrin Foundation, and Workday on verifiable credentials, and with SecureKey Technologies on a new digital identity and attribute sharing network with a mobile app, among its many collaborations.[6]

Opportunities and challenges. Concerted effort to transform obstacles into opportunities has been the most important factor in the blockchain's success thus far. Executives need to understand the regulatory uncertainty, the level of energy consumed by proof-of-work consensus mechanisms, the efforts of governments such as China and Russia to

---

3. Jai S. Arun and Alexander Carmichael. "Trust Me: Digital Identity on Blockchain." IBM Institute for Business Value, April 2017. public.dhe.ibm.com/common/ssi/ecm/gb/en/gbe03823usen/gbe03823usen-00_GBE03823USEN.pdf

4. Identity.Foundation. "Decentralized Identity Foundation" n.d. identity.foundation.

5. Identity.Foundation. "Working Groups." n.d. identity.foundation/#wgs.

6. Dan Gisolfi. "Decentralized Identity: An Alternative to Password-Based Authentication." *Blockchain Unleashed: IBM Blockchain Blog.* IBM Corporation, October 5, 2018. www.ibm.com/blogs/blockchain/2018/10/decentralized-identity-an-alternative-to-password-based-authentication; Adam Gunther. "Collaboration: Unlocking Decentralized, Digital Identity Management through Blockchain." *Blockchain Unleashed: IBM Blockchain Blog.* IBM Corporation, April 4, 2018. www.ibm.com/blogs/blockchain/2018/04/collaboration-unlocking-decentralized-digital-identity-management-through-blockchain.

limit individual use of cryptocurrencies, and the fears that blockchain
technology will be a job killer, to name a few areas of concern.
We wrote quite a bit about these issues, and we applaud the authors
for tackling them head-on.

Business models. The business models for blockchain are largely decentralized networks, subject to network effects such that when the number of
nodes increases, so does the size of the business model. Jai, Jerry, and
Nitin have described four important business models: founder-led networks, joint ventures, the consortium, and business ecosystems. They
outline a four-step process for moving from pilot project to enterprise
integration. It's very hands-on.

Governance. The blockchain space is full of formal and informal leaders.
Some have executive roles in start-up, blockchain consortia, and regulatory bodies, and others possess vision and talent that are both compelling and influential. We wrote extensively about the need for governance
networks—multistakeholder networks in the domains of standards
development, policy guidance, community advocacy, knowledge, and
education, among others. Jai, Jerry, and Nitin were wise to cast these
issues in practical terms of permissioned and permissionless blockchains, with on-chain and off-chain governance of protocols and the
applications that run on them. These issues will be critical to the scaling, interoperability, and crisis management of these systems over time.

Team building. Here's where the rubber meets the road in enterprise
blockchain pilots. IBM has vast experience in this area, assembling
teams across divisions within its own firm and working across industries and national boundaries. The authors provide a guide to getting
the right people on the team and then managing the project effectively,
so that the enterprise can leverage success and learn from failure.

Financial models. The financial services industry has become somewhat of
a Rube Goldberg contraption that performs eight basic functions: verifying identity, transferring payments, holding savings, making loans,
trading assets, investing capital, insuring assets and managing risk, and
accounting. Smart contracts and distributed applications running on
distributed ledgers are challenging incumbents in each of these eight

areas. Initial coin offerings are already disrupting venture capital. Conversely, incumbents could transform their businesses for the better, if they embrace blockchain. IBM is working directly with American International Group on a smart multinational insurance contract for Standard Chartered Bank, and with the Bank of Montreal, CaixaBank, Commerzbank, Erste Group, and UBS on their global trade finance platform called Batavia.[7]

Jai, Jerry, and Nitin have provided a sound blueprint for constructing an enterprise blockchain strategy, from identifying appropriate use cases to driving top-line growth and establishing a competitive position. We agree—now is the time for leaders to act, and *Blockchain for Business* should get them moving.

—Don Tapscott,
Cofounder and Executive Chairman
Blockchain Research Institute
Co-author, Blockchain Revolution

---

7. Suzanne Barlyn. "AIG Teams with IBM to Use Blockchain for 'Smart' Insurance Policy." *Reuters*, June 15, 2017. www.reuters.com/article/us-aig-blockchain-insurance-idUSKBN1953CD; Giulio Prisco. "IBM, Five International Banks Pilot Blockchain-Based Platform for Trade Finance." *NASDAQ.com*, April 26, 2018. www.nasdaq.com/article/ibm-five-international-banks-pilot-blockchain-based-platform-for-trade-finance-cm954045.

PREFACE

Because blockchain has the potential to drive the re-imagination of processes and business models in a distributed and decentralized manner, it can be a transformational technology for many businesses. Many business and technology leaders, however, might overlook its potential usage and value for their business and industry, or associate it primarily with Bitcoin and cryptocurrency applications.

Although blockchain is the foundational technology underpinning Bitcoin, it has broad applicability to multiple industry use cases and enables compelling value propositions beyond the financial world. The capabilities of blockchain for enterprise use cases beyond cryptocurrency are not well understood, and the potential for transforming business models in new ways by using blockchain is not obvious for many reasons. A business-driven technology usage perspective requires a balance between pragmatism and a vision for business outcomes.

WHO IS THIS BOOK FOR?

There are many good books available today that address the high-level potential of blockchain technology or go deep into technical implementation and programming topics. The primary intent of this book, however, is to address the distinct gap between high-level and deep technical concepts.

This book is a practical guide for leaders who need to understand and evaluate how blockchain technology can transform their organizations' business processes and models. It provides a simple and pragmatic overview of blockchain technology and its capabilities and value from a business perspective. It describes various real-world examples, implementation approaches, and industry-specific and cross-industry use cases. In addition, it provides leaders with the insights that are needed to define potential business models and governance structures, establish teams in decentralized or hybrid enterprises or ecosystems, and understand the costs and return of investment. Also, this book brings clarity to the current state of the technology and its evolution and describes how leaders can better prepare to take advantage of upcoming capabilities.

Many leaders who are still unsure about how to drive transformation with blockchain technology start by identifying a right business use case; defining a business model and governance structure; establishing a team; and determining costs, return on investments, and a financial structure. This book addresses these concerns for business and technology leaders by providing an integrated view of business and blockchain technology.

What Is Covered in This Book?

Our goal is to cover all of the key topics with which you need to be comfortable in order to positively impact your organization as it evaluates and implements blockchain technology. Even if you are already familiar with some of the basics, the early chapters will reinforce your understanding of important concepts and explore general use cases. As you dive deeper, you will be systematically introduced to the specific steps and details that will enable your organization to successfully implement a blockchain solution.

Feel free, however, to jump directly to the chapter that most directly impacts your current role and answers your most immediate questions. You will also find references for further study throughout the chapters to fill in any gaps or provide more detail, depending on your level of experience or organizational role.

Chapter 1: Introduction to Blockchain

The introductory content in Chapter 1 shares critical perspectives of blockchain technology so that leaders can realize its beliefs and gain a true understanding of enterprise blockchain concepts and capabilities. You will learn why blockchain matters for your business. You will learn about trailblazers and key aspects, including how to carefully select a scope for your blockchain project and motivate participants in a blockchain business network while ensuring governance. This chapter also shares some transformational examples of blockchain for social good, and shares "top of the mind" questions and answers that are related to blockchain technology.

Chapter 2: Opportunities and Challenges

You might be wondering what opportunities and challenges you might face when you implement a blockchain network. Chapter 2 describes these topics, including how blockchain can apply to your industry and business objectives. It describes how blockchain technology's disruptive elements drive transformation across traditional organizational structures, business models, and ecosystems. These elements also fundamentally open endless opportunities in many industries to innovate and challenge the status quo. The primary challenges for a blockchain project's success are specific to the scope, motivation, and governance, rather than the technology.

CHAPTER 3: UNDERSTANDING THE TECHNOLOGY LANDSCAPE

Chapter 3 defines the overall blockchain technology landscape and addresses the trust divide between an enterprise (permissioned) blockchain and a public, permissionless blockchain. Enterprise blockchain design and enterprise integration impact the cost of the solution deployment and the longevity of the application, so economic incentives are a vital component of any blockchain network. This distinction is vital for the valuation of crypto assets and to ensure the continued and sustained growth of a blockchain-powered business network.

CHAPTER 4: BUSINESS OF BUSINESS MODELS

When you are ready to adopt blockchain into your enterprise, it is important that you pick the correct business and technology model for your business and industry. You want a model that provides economic incentives for joining a blockchain network, such as the creation of value that exceeds what you can achieve alone. The correct model will also help you combat the disruptive forces that blockchain creates, which is imperative if you want to compete under this new economic paradigm. Chapter 4 describes the possible business models that you can choose, which include joint venture, consortium, NewCo, business ecosystem, Build–Own–Operate (BOO) or founder-led networks, and Build–Own–Operate–Transfer (BOOT) or founding consortium–led networks.

CHAPTER 5: DEVELOPING A GOVERNANCE STRUCTURE FOR BLOCKCHAIN NETWORKS

So, you have a model for your blockchain network and are ready to implement it. The first thing you need to do is set up a governance structure, which ensures that you and your ecosystem partners have a common vision and goals for the blockchain network. With a governance structure in place, the ecosystem partners know how their blockchain network is managed. Chapter 5 describes how to set up the governance structure, which addresses industry-specific requirements and ensures a tight linkage between the business model and the technology blueprint. By adopting a common governance structure, all participants adhere to a common set of objectives, fair and equitable use of network resources, and rules of engagement.

CHAPTER 6: BUILDING A TEAM TO DRIVE BLOCKCHAIN PROJECTS

You must gather many different people to build the team that will drive the creation of your blockchain network. Creating a blockchain project requires enterprise-level roles, such as founders, members, operators, and users, and other roles, such as steering committee members, project managers, blockchain consultants, engineers, and many more. Using "the best of the best" from each enterprise to develop a blockchain network is known as *intraprise synergy*. By using this concept, you empower each participant in the blockchain network with the decentralized authority and autonomy to use their skills as part of the broader network. Chapter 6 describes this concept and its many parts in detail.

CHAPTER 7: UNDERSTANDING FINANCIAL MODELS, INVESTMENT RUBRICS, AND MODEL RISK FRAMEWORKS

As you might have surmised by now, there are many challenges surrounding the technical complexity of blockchain. One such challenge is the plethora of financial models, investment rubrics, and frameworks (structures that aim to scale blockchain networks with the greatest efficiency) that are available today. Which do you choose? Chapter 7 helps you make that choice. By following the guidance in this chapter, you can help ensure a methodical, quantifiable, and measurable deployment of resources while effectively managing risk, all at scale. With the correct mixture of a strategic approach, business design, financial rubric, GRC framework, and access to technology acumen and the correct talent, a blockchain-powered business network can transform industries and businesses while being disruptive and immensely profitable.

CHAPTER 8: LOOKING AHEAD: WHAT DOES THE FUTURE HOLD?

This chapter prepares you for the future as the evolution of blockchain technology as the network of networks in a decentralized economy becomes more pervasive. You learn about the nexus of the blockchain technology, which includes artificial intelligence, the Internet of Things, and quantum computing, and see how these intersections can add value to your business. Also, this chapter provides readiness advice for critical areas from a futures perspective.

ACKNOWLEDGMENTS

It was an inspiring effort to find the gap in the current blockchain books out there in the market, but it was a very challenging task to fill that gap with a truly pragmatic and business value perspective. However, with the collective wisdom and more than seven decades of technology and business leadership experience, a decade of blockchain technology expertise, and thousands of customer interactions among three of us, this expedition was absolutely rewarding and heartening.

Writing a book is a journey, and during this journey there are many people who directly or indirectly help you reach your destination. We are very fortunate and sincerely thankful to have such a supportive, encouraging, and tremendous tribe, consisting of our family members, colleagues, and editing and publishing team members who graciously helped us make this journey successful.

First of all, we sincerely thank the professional and awesome publishing team from Pearson—our executive editor Gregory Doench, a great partner and pleasure to work with who made the entire book writing process very smooth and timely for us; production editor Julie Nahil; copy editor Jill Hobbs; and project manager Rachel Paul.

Second, we are indebted to many of our colleagues who provided exceptional help throughout, including Steven Stansel from IBM marketing services (previously IBM Press), who walked us through with the overall book writing process, reviewed and refined the initial book proposal, and introduced us to the Pearson team; Wade Wallace from the IBM Redbook editing team, our first-gate editor who polished the language, caught grammar inaccuracies, and filled the messaging gaps before handing it over to the Pearson team; Colby Murphy from IBM Blockchain marketing, who helped us with marketing support and specially with the looking ahead and futures content; Tim Richer and Steven Mikolajczak from IBM Blockchain marketing, who provided overall process support to ensure content sanity and adherence to marketing and legal guidelines; Peter Reith from Jerry's team, who helped him with book tasks, timing, and resources; Shaun Lynch from the IBM Blockchain design team, for the creative book cover design; and Steve Kim, also on the IBM Blockchain design team, for design consultation. Our special thanks to Marie Wieck, IBM General Manager, Blockchain, for her kind support, enabling us to work with Pearson on the book and also providing early book review and a review quote. And special thanks as well to Arvind Krishna, SVP Hybrid Cloud and Director of IBM Research, founding leader of IBM Blockchain technology, for his invaluable guidance and leadership in this space and his early book review and review quote.

Finally, we are very grateful to the following people: Don Tapscott, thought leader, author of *Blockchain Revolution*, who provided an unbiased review of the manuscript and graciously wrote the Foreword; Dr. Irving Wladawsky-Berger, technology leader and research affiliate at MIT, columnist at *WSJ CIO Journal*, and VP Emeritus, IBM, who candidly reviewed the manuscript and provided a sincere and awesome quote. To Dr. Keith Pigues, CEO and Founder of Luminas Strategy and coauthor of *Winning with Customers—a Playbook for B2B*, who provided instrumental and constructive guidance on simplifying the content and focusing on delivering value for the audience, reviewing the manuscript, and writing a review quote. To Perianne Boring, Founder and President of the Chamber of Digital Commerce, who is a driving force behind promoting the acceptance of blockchain technology through education and advocacy and working closely with governments, private organizations, policymakers, regulatory agencies, and industry—she is a great friend and leader from global blockchain community who helped us with manuscript review and provided a review quote in a timely manner.

Most importantly, Jai would like to thank, from the bottom his heart, his awesome wife, Varshal. She is a true inspiration and sparked his thoughts and encouraged him to write the book. While working herself full-time as senior program manager for information privacy and security at Cisco Systems, she did double duty for several months taking care of everything at home: their two young children's school, club, and sports activities many evenings, and over weekends by herself for all the piano, dance, taekwondo, and painting classes, and soccer, basketball, and volleyball practices and games. Thank you so much, darling. Jai would like to extend his thanks to his daughter, Saachi, and his son, Yogya, for their understanding and for allowing Daddy to spend ample time to write this book, missing many great moments of their activities. Also, Jai is eternally grateful to his mother, Saroopi Devi; father, Phusiya Ram; and mother-in-law, Chitra Mayekar, who have been calling him from India every other day during this period, asking about his well-being and showering their blessings on him. Jai and Varshal's siblings from India—Suchita, Ramesh, Amey, Vijay, Sunita, Anita, and Vinita—have been a great support and motivational backbone.

Beside Jai's family, of course, this would not have been possible without his coauthors. He truly enjoyed this memorable book-writing experience shared with them and sincerely thanks Jerry for his extraordinary leadership and technology vision. He thanks Nitin for bringing unique insights and true balance from his hundreds of client interactions to the critical topics of the book. Finally, he appreciates and thanks his management team, including Bruce Hawks, Venkat Raghavan, and Sanjay Tripathy, for their direct and indirect motivation and support.

In the spirit of Jerry famously saying, "Blockchain is a team sport," Jerry would like to acknowledge Team Cuomo: starting with his lovely wife, Stephanie; his dad and mom, Jerome/Pop and Rita/Reetz; his daughter and son-in-law, Rose/Robo and Christophe B.; his son, Gennaro/Bud; his sisters, Stephanie/Ses and Andrea/Agia; and his many wonderful in-laws, aunts, uncles, nieces, nephews, and cousins. Each person has helped shaped Jerry's smile. He thanks the Mind the Gap band (Aydo, Barry, Marc, and Lin) for putting up with practices he missed.

And "Blockchain Jerry" would not be that without his workmates. He knows that by only naming a few, he will get in trouble for leaving people off the list, but he has to, at least, thank the current leadership team of the "IBM chain gang" that supported him in getting blocks on the ledger: Arvind K., Marie W., Bridget Van K., Ramesh G., Brigid M., James W., John McLean, Gari S., Krishna R., Chris F., Sharon C., Anthony O., Kathryn H., Mark P., Peter R., Andy C., Bobbie C., Meeta, Mihir S., David H., Gale F., Steve K., Tim R., Alan D., Alan B., Adam G., Dan G., Eileen L., Rob S., Rachel J., and Michael B. . . . and John W. Jerry has special thanks for Colby Murphy for helping guide his pen in the right direction. Last but not least, Jerry thanks his coauthors, Jai and Nitin, for ensuring that when Jerry agreed to help write this book, it was treated as a transaction on the blockchain that once committed could not be undone. This team has defined Jerry and made him who he is today—and he is so thankful for that.

Nitin would like to acknowledge his wife, Ritu, for her support and for handling things on the home front and taking care of their son, Neil. While jobs and related travel can be extremely demanding on everyone's time, writing a book adds to the ordeal. It is at such times that a nudge and encouragement can do wonders for energy levels, so he thanks both Ritu and Neil for supporting him through this journey.

Also, he would to thank his coauthors: Jerry for his mentorship, leadership, and support, and Jai for shepherding him through the process and making sure every single detail was covered. He also thanks Tim Richer from IBM Marketing for his support, Wade Wallace for an early draft edit, and Jill from the Pearson team for timely edits and responses. Special thanks to Greg Doench from Pearson for his guidance on the publication process.

About the Authors

 **Jai Singh Arun** is a senior program director at IBM's corporate strategy team and drives strategic product management and business development of IBM Research innovations within the areas of blockchain, artificial intelligence, and cybersecurity. He has over two decades of global, cross-functional business and emerging technologies leadership experience, building multi-million dollar software, systems, and services businesses.

 **Jerry Cuomo** leads IBM's engineering and product initiatives on Blockchain. He holds the prestigious title of IBM Fellow and is recognized as one of the most prolific contributors to IBM's software business, producing products and technologies that have profoundly impacted how the industry conducts commerce over the World Wide Web.

 **Nitin Gaur** is an IBM distinguished engineer and worldwide director and leads IBM's global blockchain labs and services. He is responsible for strategy and for developing IBM's digital currency technologies and offerings, such as stable coins and digital fiat. He pioneered IBM's enterprise blockchain strategy and advised IBM decision makers, business partners, and clients on the use of the technology.

1

Introduction to Blockchain

Blockchain will do for transactions what the Internet did for information.

—Ginni Rometty, CEO, IBM

Blockchain is a technology that is poised to usher in a new way of conducting business that will change everyday life for the better. Blockchain empowers groups of institutions to achieve better outcomes by creating new growth opportunities that together are greater than the feats that any single member could achieve alone.

Blockchain makes it possible to reimagine many of the world's most fundamental business interactions and opens the door to new styles of digital interactions yet to be imagined. It is now regularly showing its potential to vastly reduce the cost and complexity of getting things done across industries, government agencies, and social institutions.

Most people who have heard of blockchain associate it with the cryptocurrency Bitcoin. Although they are related, these two concepts are not the same. The potential uses for blockchain are far broader than the applications for cryptocurrency. Also, whereas the Bitcoin network operates on permissionless membership principles and extends anonymity, a permissioned blockchain network governs its membership with known entities.

The full benefits of blockchain will be realized through its broadest use across the broadest set of industries. We have participated in hundreds of blockchain projects across the supply chain government, healthcare, transportation, insurance, chemicals and petroleum, and many more industries. From those experiences, we have developed three key beliefs.

BLOCKCHAIN BELIEFS

We have the following beliefs about blockchain that reveal its vast promise:

- **Transformative:** We believe that blockchain is a transformative technology that can radically change the way businesses interact. At the center of a blockchain is a shared immutable ledger. Each member of a blockchain network has an exact copy of the ledger that is kept current as it updates over time. After a transaction is entered, it cannot be changed. With this shared copy of the truth:
  - **Net new growth opportunities are discovered** because new trusted business models are identified.
  - **Sustainable competitive advantage is gained** through participation in a new decentralized economy with new business models.
  - **Time is saved** because multiparty transactions can be processed immediately.
  - **Costs are reduced** because overhead is eliminated by having businesses transact directly with each other.
  - **Risk is mitigated** because the ledger acts as an immutable audit trail.
- **Open:** We believe that blockchain must be open to encourage broad adoption, innovation, and interoperability. Organizations such as the Linux Foundation's Hyperledger Project, with hundreds of members across all industries, have provided a breeding ground for business-savvy

blockchain software. Only with openness will blockchain be widely adopted and spur innovation for business.

- **Ready for business:** We believe that blockchain is ready for business use today. A new breed of blockchain technology is now available that has been engineered from the ground up, under the governance of the Hyperledger Project, to handle the demands of enterprises and provide a foundation that ensures good ethical business behavior.

ENTERPRISE BLOCKCHAIN

The basic blockchain concept can be defined quite simply: It is a shared, decentralized, cryptographically secured, and immutable digital ledger. However, *enterprise* blockchain enriches this definition with a few key attributes:

- **Accountability:** Network members are *known* and identified by cryptographic membership keys with assigned access permissions by business role. Without such accountability, compliance with regulations such as the Health Insurance Portability and Accountability Act of 1996 (HIPAA) and General Data Protection Regulation of 2018 (GDPR) would be nearly impossible to achieve.

- **Privacy:** Although members are known to the network, transactions are shared only with those members that need to know about them. Enterprise blockchain uses various techniques to achieve privacy, including peer-to-peer[1] connections, privacy channels,[2] and zero-knowledge proofs.[3]

- **Scalability:** Supporting an immense volume of transactions is critical to enterprise scenarios. Because transactions are not typically throttled in enterprise blockchains as they are in networks like Bitcoin, they can be carried out immediately. Any particular enterprise's transaction rates will depend on many factors, including the number of peers and the complexity of the smart contract. Transaction rates measured in thousands of transactions per second are certainly achievable.[4]

- The Event Ticketing[10] solution that is convened by True Tickets
- The Autonomous Car[11] solution that is convened by Car eWallet
- The Internet of Loyalty[12] that is convened by Loyyal

These solutions are real, running applications—not proofs-of-concepts. They serve as production systems with multiple members, adding blocks and exchanging value daily.

FOUNDERS

The trailblazers who founded these networks have many things in common. Most notably, behind these solutions you will find a set of imaginative individuals who exemplify the dominant connector archetype.[13] For instance, Greg Wolfond[14] from SecureKey has an inclusive personality and naturally promotes a culture of working together toward a common goal. As a solution convener, Greg has maven and salesman archetype qualities, which instills in others the excitement and motivation to participate in a multi-institutional solution working toward a mantra of "The group can produce a better outcome than any individual institution alone."

By working closely with these solution founders and following trends that are observed from hundreds of blockchain engagements, we have learned what it takes to move an idea to a live network. Specifically, these founders have balanced scope, incentives, and governance to produce a live network.

SCOPE: DREAM LARGE AND ACT INCREMENTALLY

Blockchain solution founders *dream large* and *act incrementally*. They aim to unleash the transformative power of blockchain, but realize that their "moon shot" requires an "Apollo program" that lays out a set of steps that ultimately move the solution to production.

Trailblazing founders agree that the solution scope must be *business-driven*. Most founders set goals that are disruptive, leading to a new way of conducting business. At the same time, their minimal viable product

(*MVP*) goal is more basic, usually focused on demonstrating one facet of the disruptive business model, which is more likely to yield an initial cost savings versus a new revenue stream for solution members. Rather than "ripping and replacing," some founders initially keep their current business-to-business systems in place while they run their distributed ledger technology in parallel to add new functions to an existing business process; in doing so, this approach enriches—rather than replaces—the process. We call this a "shadow ledger."

Similarly, although successful solution founders realize that a decentralized solution is the goal, only a minimal viable ecosystem (*MVE*) of members must participate to launch the solution. Solutions that commence with more members take longer to activate than solutions that start with fewer members. Membership considerations are critical and must be addressed up front. New members might be hesitant to join a network in which their competitors are also participating. However, having competitors participate makes the ecosystem more trusted and vibrant because trust is gained through a diversity of members. The right governance and incentive system can help.

MOTIVATION: DRIVING MOMENTUM WITHIN THE ECOSYSTEM

Successful founders understand how to *motivate the members of their network*. This motivation is often accomplished by creating an economy of buyers (data consumers) and sellers (data providers) within the solution. Motivation is created by balancing obligations and rewards.

For example, the SecureKey solution provides "privacy protecting" ground rules (defined in chaincode) for how data are exchanged. This set of rules also ensures that digital asset providers "get paid" when digital asset consumers "pay" to have identity attributes verified. The ground rules create the backbone of a digital marketplace, which motivates participation through better accuracy, lower-cost verification, greater speed, and a better overall user experience.

Asset tokenization is an emerging technique that is used by enterprise blockchain founders to provide a motivational incentive system. In many cases, the token is native to the solution and can play a role akin to that of loyalty points. For example, one solution introduces a native carbon credit token that is awarded to a network member when that user conserves energy. The user can exchange the token for discounts on debit card purchases that are made via a debit card provider that, like the local energy company, is also a network member.

GOVERNANCE: THE TOTAL IS GREATER THAN THE SUM OF THE PARTS

Governance is mandatory within a blockchain network, and a blockchain solution's likelihood to go live is increased to the degree it is written down. The best founders are "referees" who bring together the group on multiple levels. In each case, a "board of stakeholders" is convened to define the rules that are inherent in the solutions and converge on the scope and motivation.

Workgroups are typically defined to focus on business models, legal concerns regarding intellectual property (IP) rights and liability, technical design, and architecture. Proper business governance encourages participation and removes uncertainty and the risk of business obligations (which are embodied in smart contracts). Proper technical governance ensures that the blockchain solution can be managed in a decentralized way so that deployment of new smart contracts or the invitation of new members happens with consent from the group.

The first graduating class of blockchain trailblazers has already had their solutions go live, with "blocks on the chain." They are dreaming large but starting incrementally, motivating a group of diverse members to participate in a solution through incentives and an inclusive governance process.

BLOCKCHAIN FOR GOOD

The trust model that underlies blockchain networks provides a natural setting for solutions that are unmatched in delivering social good. Blockchain is poised to deliver strong business returns. Moreover, when used correctly, it can deliver user experiences that are respectful of user privacy and literally save lives.

Here are three examples that illustrate how blockchain for social good is also good for business.

REDUCING FOODBORNE ILLNESSES

Has this ever happened to you? You are rushing through New York's LaGuardia Airport trying to make a flight. You are hungry and grab a salad before hopping on the plane. An hour into the flight, though, you do not feel well.

In 2006, a nationwide outbreak of *Escherichia coli*[15] was linked to bagged spinach. It took regulators two weeks to conduct the backtrace and determine the exact source of the outbreak. During those two weeks, many people got sick and one person died. Tons of good spinach was unnecessarily discarded—wrongfully wasted—because we could not tell the good spinach from the bad.

IBM Food Trust Network[16] consists of several major food companies, including Walmart, Unilever, and Nestlé. This network enables supply chain visibility across these members (and their ecosystem) to quickly pinpoint the sources of contamination. The network is already showing results that can reduce the impact of food recalls and limit the number of people who get sick or die from foodborne illnesses.

With blockchain, network members can track the provenance of ingredients as they travel from farm to fork. Recently, Walmart did an experiment that traced the origin of sliced mangos from Walmart stores back to the farm.

syrups for children that contain powerful opioids, and fake antimalarial pills made of only potato and cornstarch.

The Crypto Anchor Verifier project[20] from IBM Research Lab aims to use artificial intelligence (AI) technology with blockchain to prevent counterfeiting. The technology uniquely identifies a physical asset as a corresponding digital asset to trace provenance. The manufacturer can place a digital cryptographic fingerprint of an aspirin on a blockchain so that the pill can be verified for authenticity as it progresses across the supply chain.

The Crypto Anchor Verifier provides a lens attachment for a standard smartphone. This app leverages AI technology to perform light spectral analysis against a physical asset. It captures microscopic properties, viscosity, and other identifiers, and produces a unique digital identifier for physical goods. When immutably placed on a blockchain, the "fingerprint" of that digital good can be checked again by the Crypto Anchor Verifier at customs, at a point of purchase, or immediately before you swallow your medication.

These examples show the promise of blockchain. It is energizing to see blockchain changing everyday life for social good. With this benefit as a motivation, we continue to solve the business and technical problems that will unleash many similarly inspiring uses of an enterprise blockchain.[21]

BLOCKCHAIN QUESTIONS FROM BUSINESS AND TECHNOLOGY LEADERS

Blockchain is both a disruptive technology and a transformational one. As you think about leveraging blockchain for your business, you might have several questions in mind. As we have shared the blockchain technology and its business value with hundreds of business and technology leaders from many different industries, a predominant set of questions emerged. We did our research and rounded up the most searched terms as they relate to blockchain for business. Figure 1.1 shows these terms and their associated volume of interest.

Figure 1.1 Most searched blockchain for business terms.

After observing the data from our study, we inferred the top six questions that business leaders might have about blockchain. Each of these questions is introduced here and explored in further detail throughout the rest of this book.

DOES BLOCKCHAIN APPLY TO MY INDUSTRY AND BUSINESS OBJECTIVES?

Blockchain will most certainly impact every industry, including yours. In many cases, blockchain solutions will affect specific industries and cross-industries. For example, the trade, financial, and food-supply industries already are connected by blockchain. Blockchain will transform the way many industries do business, but it will not be the answer for every business objective.

open technologies or open source, and even enterprise platforms like IBM Blockchain offer free tiers to help you get started.

OTHER QUESTIONS

Here are some other questions that might be of interest as ponder enterprise blockchain. All these questions will be covered as you continue through this book.

- What are the advantages of adopting blockchain?
- What are the top challenges in implementing blockchain?
- Are there guides to help with implementing blockchain?
- Which scalability concerns arise with blockchain?
- Which type of IT infrastructure is needed to implement blockchain?
- How do I think about designing a blockchain solution?
- Which speed and data acceleration factors must be addressed to meet transactional requests?

CHAPTER SUMMARY

We hope that this introductory chapter has piqued your curiosity about blockchain and its enormous benefits. Imagine a world where your data are secure, fewer people die due to foodborne illnesses, and counterfeiting is a worthless endeavor due to the instant verification of fakes—to name just a few of the benefits of blockchain.

If these benefits are not enough for you, think about how your business can benefit from showing accountability to governments and other entities, safeguarding its business moves while remaining efficient, scaling the enterprise to new levels, keeping its data accessible while also keeping it secure, and profiting from contributing data to the blockchain network.

If this sounds amazing to you and you are eager to learn more about the opportunities that are provided by a blockchain network, continue with

Chapter 2. It explores more of the opportunities that blockchain can create for your enterprise, but also highlights some of the challenges that you must overcome to reap its copious and profitable benefits.

REFERENCES

1. "Security Model." *The Network: R3 Corda V3.0 Documentation*. R3, 2016. docs.corda.net/releases/release-M8.2/key-concepts-security-model.html.

2. "Channels." *Prerequisites: Hyperledger–Fabric Docs Master Documentation*. Hyperledger, 2017. hyperledger-fabric.readthedocs.io/en/release-1.0/channels.html.

3. "Zero-Knowledge Proof Standardization." An Open Industry/Academic Initiative, 2019. zkproof.org/.

4. Vukolic, Marko. "IBM Research: Behind the Architecture of Hyperledger Fabric." *The Analytics Maturity Model (IT's Best Kept Secret Is Optimization)*. IBM, 2018. www.ibm.com/blogs/research/2018/02/architecture-hyperledger-fabric/.

5. Ongaro, Diego, and John Ousterhout. "In Search of an Understandable Consensus Algorithm (Consensus Version." raft.github.io/raft.pdf.

6. Center for Food Safety and Applied Nutrition. "Labeling & Nutrition: Changes to the Nutrition Facts Label." *U.S. Food and Drug Administration*, Center for Drug Evaluation and Research, 2018. www.fda.gov/Food/GuidanceRegulation/GuidanceDocumentsRegulatoryInformation/LabelingNutrition/ucm385663.htm.

7. Condon, Mairin. "We.Trade Blockchain Platform Completes Multiple Real-Time Customer Transactions." We.Trade, 2018. we-trade.com/article/we-trade-blockchain-platform-completes-multiple-real-time-customer-transactions.

8. "Your Identity in Your Control." Verified.Me, SecureKey Technologies, 2018. verified.me/.

9. "CLSNet." Oversight Committee, CLS Group, 2018. www.cls-group.com/products/processing/clsnet/.

shared or peer-to-peer economy for every industry and organization, including intermediaries, to reimagine and transform their business processes and business models. However, every opportunity comes with an initial challenge. Blockchain adoption is challenging when you try to address too large a scope, there are no motivations or incentives for participants, and the governance structure is cumbersome and has many stakeholders.

DISRUPTIVE ELEMENTS

What makes blockchain so disruptive? Blockchain intrinsically bridges the trust gap in our business networks and our societies by co-developing a shared copy of the truth. Five critical elements of the blockchain technology drive this disruption: transparency, immutability, security, consensus, and smart contracts (Figure 2.1). How you see these disruptive elements—that is, your perspective of each of them—suggests ways to transform your business.

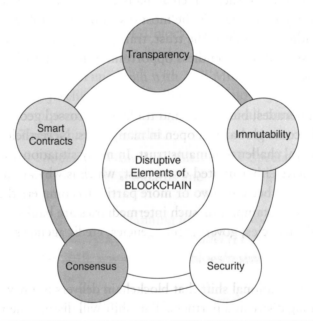

Figure 2.1 The five disruptive elements of blockchain technology.

TRANSPARENCY

Blockchain provides end-to-end visibility of your business transactions with a single source of truth that is replicated or shared across the distributed ledger in your business network. Based on the permissions that are given in a private or public blockchain-based business network, you can see the full trail of a transaction. In the past, this transparency has not existed in business networks that involve multiple participants. Thus, the new transparency disrupts many intermediaries or third parties in your business network by enabling direct peer-to-peer connection and exchange.

Imagine a supply chain network with a single source of truth across the value chain.

It is difficult to get real-time visibility of shipments in a logistics and supply-chain business because such a complex network includes multiple participants (users of goods, retailers, distributors, manufacturers, suppliers, and brokers), each of which keeps its own record of a transaction, and whose records are never synchronized. A blockchain-based supply chain network provides greater visibility and transparency that drives efficiency and higher value.

IMMUTABILITY

After you record a transaction into a blockchain, no one can delete it. If you try to modify the transaction, the blockchain appends another update record to the transaction, which is visible to the participants in the network. Each transaction in a blockchain is encoded into a data block and uniquely signed and timestamped. Each block is connected to the blocks before and after it. These blocks cannot be altered or modified; they are linked together to form a chain that is immutable and irreversible. An immutable history of transactions eliminates the counterfeiting and fraud challenges faced by many businesses.

The blockchain-driven provenance process eradicates counterfeiting by using immutability and transparency.

Counterfeiting is the biggest challenge globally for legal and financial documents and valuable goods, such as drugs, food products, luxury clothes, and jewelry. It costs companies more than 7 percent of their annual expenditures, amounting to almost $4 trillion each year on a global scale.[1] The immutable digital record and history of transfer of an asset or good are identifiable and visible to the participants within the blockchain network, so this approach blocks fraud and tampering attempts in a system or process.

SECURITY

Blockchain provides a highly secure transaction system that is almost impossible to hack. Every transaction record on a blockchain is cryptographically secured with digital signatures, along with a trail of the transaction updates. Participants in the network have their own private keys that are assigned to a transaction or any update to an existing transaction. Therefore, security vulnerabilities are easily identified and inherently prevented. Every transaction is replicated or shared across the distributed ledger, which means that hackers must look at every ledger and find the same data or record across all the ledgers, which is difficult.

Security, privacy, and compliance are bolstered by a distributed ledger, transaction integrity, high availability, and auditability.

The security of business-critical data and transactions is a primary concern in any organization and across all industries. Digital transformation of such data and transactions, in turn, is the key driving force of further complexity in today's business world and brings up new security issues. Global cybersecurity spending was expected to exceed $114 billion in 2018, according to analyst firm Gartner,[2] and Statista predicts that it will total more than $234 billion by 2022.[3]

Most organizations keep their business and customer information in a centralized system. Unfortunately, such centralized systems are vulnerable to attack. Blockchain applies a decentralized approach, in which the transaction data are replicated across the distributed ledger. Thus, even though one of the ledgers is not active, the other ledgers have a copy of the transactions and ensure availability. Each transaction is validated or consented to by network participants before it is posted in the ledger. Although you can identify the members in a blockchain, they can maintain their anonymity and privacy, which is important for organizations to ensure trust. Having an untampered transaction history in blockchain delivers readily available auditability for compliance and regulation purposes.

Consensus

The network participants in blockchain use a consensus mechanism to eliminate the need to rely on central authorities and third parties to validate business transactions. The foundation of cryptocurrency, for example, is a public blockchain that requires miners to validate the currency transactions. This process, which is called *proof of work* or *mining overhead*, involves a huge amount of computing power and energy. In contrast, permissioned blockchain includes trusted participants on the network and uses consensus algorithms that validate transactions anonymously without mining overhead, and with a fraction of the computing power and the energy costs that are used in a public blockchain.

Consensus drives fair participation in a business network with democracy.

On a global scale, unfairness is more than 50% in economic structures where benefits and burdens are not fairly distributed across the country government according to a BBC poll. Many businesses spend billions of dollars every year to deal with unfairness issues, while others lose billions of dollars every year without being aware of unfairness. Many intermediaries in the legal, business, and government arenas take advantage of unfairness and deceptive practices for their own economic or financial benefits. Blockchain technology has the potential to replace the unfairness in government and businesses with a truly democratic and transparent approach toward transactions.

SMART CONTRACTS

You can think of smart contracts as self-executing electronic contracts that state the legal and business terms of an agreement between business partners. Smart contracts in blockchain are business logics that are programmed and embedded into a transaction record that enable business process automation. Such contracts allow transactions and agreements to be executed among various business participants without engaging the services of a central authority, legal system, or arbitrator. Business process automation is possible by using smart contracts because the transactions in blockchain are trusted, transparent, and immutable.

Smart contracts fuel business process innovation with automation, speed, and compliance without hefty costs and risks.

Even though automation and agility are increasing in business or legal contracts management, the average cost of processing and reviewing a basic contract has increased by 38 percent in the last six years and now averages $6900, according to the International Association for Contract and Commercial Management (IACCM).[4] The global legal services market alone is expected to top $1 trillion by 2021, based on a Statista report.[5] Think how much you are spending on your contract management services and how much potential smart contracts have to save money, enable contracts to be processed faster or almost instantaneously electronically, and reduce risks through application of transparency and immutability. Initial estimates suggest that blockchain technology can reduce the execution time of business contracts from days to minutes, from manual to automated, at a fraction of the current cost, essentially without any legal entity becoming involved.

Next, we'll explore how these disruptive elements from blockchain can uncover new opportunities for your business's transformation.

OPPORTUNITIES

Many individuals and organizations (sometimes unintentionally) thwart positive changes in business due to their inability to see how new innovative technologies can revolutionize the future. Emerging technologies bring new opportunities and change our lives by changing the way that we think and operate. Two of the revolutionary technologies that we witnessed in the 20th century were personal computers and the Internet. The next significant transformative technology of the 21st century is blockchain.

Gartner forecasts that the business value that is driven by blockchain will amount to $3.1 trillion by 2030.[6] The true business value will be driven by the new opportunities that users envision to transform their businesses in various use cases across a wide range of industries, from cryptocurrency to cross-border payments, food safety to provenance, supply chain to trade finance, clinical trials to healthcare exchanges, digital rights management to royalty settlements, digital identity to land registry, and many more. Blockchain presents endless opportunities.

TRANSFORMATIVE POWER OF BLOCKCHAIN

Blockchain technology drives transformational opportunities in three ways so that enterprises, economies, and ecosystems flourish. This transformation trilogy is composed of new organizational structures, new business models, and new ecosystems (Figure 2.2).

Organizations' brand and reputation systems that are built on blockchain can provide assurance of truth and transparency through their business records, which can visibly demonstrate trustworthiness to their potential clients and partners.

Examples of such business model transformations include the following:

- A music distribution model in which music files are exchanged directly from creator to the listeners and monetized without any distributors
- A remittance model in which money is transferred from a sender to a receiver without a financial institution acting as an intermediary
- An open market model that connects buyers and sellers directly without an exchange intermediary

Decentralized Ecosystem

An open approach toward business transactions' trust and transparency in a network that is driven by blockchain promotes a transformational journey for the network's participants. In this approach, organizations and systems cooperate, and value is co-created and contained in the network.

As blockchain delivers distributed organizational structures and trusted business models, it fosters new emerging trusted marketplaces and economy-to-exchange value. Peer-to-peer models are driving the new ecosystem of players and eliminated the roles for intermediaries. This systematic change fosters the creation of new consumers, competitors, microeconomies, profit pools, and a distributed ecosystem. Decentralized, ecosystem-driven markets are impossible to compete with.

The following examples illustrate new ecosystems that can emerge as part of distributed environments:

- Start-up funding is reinvented by using initial coin offerings (ICO) and tokens.

- A "know your customers" (KYC) service is created and used within a business network and eliminates the traditional KYC that was redundant for each organization.
- Assets and land registration in developing nations can leapfrog traditional rural and urban development and real estate governance ecosystems in developed nations.
- A trading and investment model runs without a clearinghouse.

Achieving these kinds of advances is not a matter of mastering the blockchain technology; instead, it requires rethinking your current market role, value streams, and existing business ecosystems, and finding opportunities to transform your business. This is a new radical shift in businesses in which many elements must be redesigned, such as organizational structure, business model, and ecosystem.

TRANSFORMATIVE OPPORTUNITIES

This section examines some of the industry-specific transformational opportunities that may be driven by blockchain, beyond Bitcoin or cryptocurrency.

Banking and Financial Markets

Blockchain capabilities deliver banking innovations to revamp the experience for customers by reducing transaction times from hours to seconds, eliminating manual processes, and eradicating unnecessary intermediaries in trade finance, digital identities, and cross-border payments. With blockchain, you can conduct business rapidly and securely, moving from paper-based to blockchain-stored transaction records, which can enable easier expansion to underserved markets, such as small and medium enterprises.

Trade Finance

Banks continue to struggle with manual processes and stringent requirements for managing, tracking, and securing domestic and cross-border trade transactions. For example, processes for corporate trade financing letters of credit are typically paper based and fragmented, which can make financing more challenging for the 50 percent of smaller enterprises that might not have credit sources.

Blockchain-based smart contracts can automatically store, secure, and exchange contract details and financial terms; coordinate trade logistics and payments via an integrated real-time network; and streamline digital trade processes. With blockchain, ledger transactions can flow from one small enterprise to another one through a trusted bank. Larger firms can also benefit by better tracking of trade finance transactions.

For example, IBM and eight European banks have created We.Trade, which is a multiple-bank collaboration that is building trusted digital trade chain connections with smaller enterprises.

Digital Identity Verification

Requiring clients to repeatedly provide identifying information can erode customer satisfaction and cause transaction delays. Onboarding clients for checking accounts or mortgages or migrating them from one bank to another requires strict compliance with KYC standards.

On IBM Blockchain, identification documentation can be consolidated with managed access and permissions without storing the actual identifying information. This supports KYC due diligence, helps secure personal information, and enhances client satisfaction.

For example, IBM and SecureKey Technologies are building an identity-sharing ecosystem with Canadian banks that will enable clients to instantly verify identities when opening new accounts. Other uses include driver's license applications and requests for utility services.

Insurance

Blockchain can simplify and secure multiparty operations at the heart of the insurance industry. Whether interacting with customers or dealing with other parties, blockchain can reduce the challenges that are presented by multiple parties that keep their own records.

As transactions occur, insurers can rely on blockchain's distributed ledger technology to update and validate information against other records in the network; reduce management costs for policies, claims, and relationships; streamline operations; and enhance customer satisfaction. Companies can also capture opportunities and revenue through new business models or new insurance products.

Complex Risk Coverage

Employees, policy holders, adjusters, and agents who cannot view insurance policy information usually need human help, which increases the chance of errors, delays claims resolution, and increases costs. The challenge escalates with complex insurance programs or managing policies in multiple countries, which can involve strict legal and regulatory adherence. Blockchain can resolve many of these obstacles to smooth operations.

For example, using IBM Blockchain, AIG and Standard Chartered converted multiple policies into "smart contracts" that provided a single, consolidated view of policy data and documentation in real time. The solution enables visibility into coverage and premium payments, delivering automated notifications to network participants after payment events occur.

Group Benefits

Organizations offering group benefits often rely on a complex network of administrators, providers, employees, and others to manage those benefits. Different versions of the same data require consolidation to ensure eligibility and access to benefits.

For example, IBM Blockchain can be the vital link across a vast ecosystem of third-party administrators and service provider networks. Its shared ledger transparency can help employers reduce errors, which results in improved claims processing, better provider management, and lower operational expenses.

Healthcare

Blockchain can transform healthcare enterprises and increase the quality of care by enabling new ecosystems and new business models to evolve. Healthcare information that is stored on a blockchain can change the way that providers store clinical information and how they share information within their own organization as well as with other healthcare partners, payers, and patients.

Blockchain decentralizes healthcare information, increasing data availability, efficiency, transparency, and trust. However, it requires careful planning to make the most of the advantages it brings. The blockchain infrastructure that IBM is helping to build provides enterprises with a solid platform for both immediate and long-term business solutions.

Patient Consent and Health Data Exchange

Disparate record-keeping systems can result in patient consent forms and medical histories that are incomplete, conflicting, or ambiguous. By comparison, blockchain-stored records can be used to provide complete, longitudinal health records for individuals, giving all patients more control over their own information through verifiable consent. With blockchain, every patient record reflects the best-known medical facts, from genomics data to diagnostic medical imaging, and data can be reliably transferred when needed, with no need for a central gatekeeper.

Clinical Trials Management

Clinical trials of healthcare interventions generate mountains of data, which requires healthcare administrators to keep reliable and consistent records for peer review and to meet regulatory requirements. Blockchain tools, in concert with electronic data capture (EDC), allows clinical data to be automatically aggregated, replicated, and distributed among researchers and practitioners with greater auditability, provenance tracking, and control compared to complicated conventional systems.

Retail and Consumer Goods

Blockchain is removing obstacles and increasing visibility for consumer products and retail business transactions. Greater transparency through a shared and immutable ledger enables businesses to establish a climate of trust across areas such as invoicing and payments, the consumer supply chain, and global shipping. Through the use of a distributed and trusted database, a blockchain solution reduces barriers that might otherwise impede business, such as siloed management and regulatory systems, time-consuming settlement processes, and uncertainty between entities conducting transactions.

Blockchain speeds transactions, builds trust between participating members, and opens the door to cross-industry and global business opportunities.

Commerce

All too often, lengthy invoicing and payment processes across diverse systems lead to delays in verification and payments, triggering disputes and driving up the cost of doing business in today's global markets. Blockchain helps remove friction from such commerce by providing a common chain of information visibility that is shared across vendors and purchasers.

For example, a major consumer goods company used IBM Blockchain to reduce the complexity and ambiguity it encountered in invoice processing. The solution cut processing times from five days to one and trimmed processing costs by 50 percent. The company plans to expand its new model to numerous other supplier relationships.

need for multiple stakeholders in advertising purchases and digital content management. With an immutable and shared ledger that records transactions as they occur, companies in media, advertising, entertainment, and others have complete visibility as content or data are purchased and used.

Blockchain is designed to accelerate the creation of "built for business" global blockchain networks across industries and use cases. The implications for media and entertainment can be profound, such as in digital rights management—trusted and transparent content distribution in a digital ecosystem.

Advertisement Settlement

Nearly 50 percent of ads fail to reach their intended audience.[7] Moreover, antiquated rating and measurement systems can make it impossible to know the precise number of audience impressions achieved with a specific ad. Digital advertising fraud costs at least $7 billion annually,[8] while intermediaries profit from 60 percent of ad spending. Discrepancies in systems of record typically lead to disputes, labor costs, leakage, and poor cash flow.

Using an immutable blockchain ledger can remove the need for intermediaries, thereby reducing advertising costs. By digitally recording transactions across the advertising ecosystem, advertisers, intermediaries, and advertising sellers have a shared knowledge of impressions and can use smart contracts to create a transparent system that proves spending is based on actual impressions. Inventory management can be streamlined, and billing and invoicing can become more efficient for agencies creating ads.

For example, Unilever, one of the world's largest advertisers, partnered with IBM to build a blockchain solution to manage its advertising supply chain and create a trust-based and transparent solution that enables buyer verification, offering a way for all parties to visualize every part of the advertising process. The new transparency will make it easier for advertisers and advertising platforms to know how efficient campaigns are, justifying (or not) advertising expenses.

Loyalty Programs

Loyalty programs have been implemented in a variety of forums, spanning the hospitality, finance, entertainment, airline, and retail industries, among others. However, segmented systems can make it impossible for consumers to exchange their loyalty points across entities, including ones in the same industry, such as banks. This situation limits cross-marketing and revenue growth opportunities.

Blockchain solutions make it possible to provide complete visibility into a loyalty inventory to establish trust across the loyalty ecosystem, enabling, for example, a consumer to book a hotel, purchase a theme park ticket, or buy a cup of coffee by using frequent-flyer points. Conversely, the consumer can gain credit through loyalty points that are earned with other entities and use them with the airline.

For example, China UnionPay, which guarantees credit card usage across Chinese banks in more than 150 countries, uses IBM Blockchain to help bank customers exchange bonus points that are earned through purchases among disparate banks. The new peer-to-peer bank reward point trading system will allow points exchange between banks, credit card users, and gift shops.

Automotive

Every part of the complex automotive business ecosystem—from parts suppliers and manufacturers to customers and safety regulators—relies on a network of transactions and knowledge that starts long before a vehicle is manufactured and extends far beyond its purchase. That network is growing. From support for evolving hardware and services to understanding the provenance and location of defective or counterfeit parts, the amount of data that the automotive industry must track is exploding.

visibility into the common information that is necessary for settling disputes over pay, work status, or other issues that might arise.

Cargo Handling

Shipping goods involves multiple parties, including senders, receivers, carriers, and regulators. Given the involvement of so many entities, each with a different records system, blockchain can help track the location and condition of cargo. Using shared records of ownership, location, and movement, carriers can improve their load utilization, and senders and receivers can speed delivery by clearing customs in transit instead of waiting at the terminal.

For example, dnata (Dubai National Air Transport Association), a global provider of ground handling, cargo, travel, and flight catering services for more than 400 airlines, teamed with IBM to eliminate redundant data and improve visibility and transparency for cargo services by using blockchain. The results streamlined and simplified the processes from the point of origin to the final destination. The blockchain solution achieves this task by digitizing the supply chain and by using a peer-to-peer network to manage and track each cargo container's path.

CHALLENGES

The primary challenges with the application of blockchain are not about having a perfect and matured technology: The evolution of blockchain technology will undoubtedly continue, much as Internet technology continues to advance nearly four decades after its first introduction. Blockchain technology has been used for several years as an underlying foundation for cryptocurrency application, and lately many organizations have advanced it to ensure its enterprise readiness for other industries. The key challenges are choosing the right scope, having the right motivation for a business and its participants, ensuring the right governance structure, and having the correct team and technology in place. These challenges can be conquered if you make deliberate and diligent efforts to manage the blockchain network effectively and focus on driving the ultimate transformation that you envisioned.

As shown in Figure 2.3, addressing the challenges involves three aspects: The scope helps you determine what plan you should make for a blockchain network, governance defines how you should operate it, and motivation drives why you should build or participate in it.

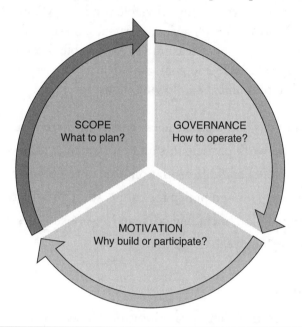

Figure 2.3 Addressing the challenges.

SCOPE

Although blockchain has the potential to disrupt many businesses, current business policies and requirements might not immediately support the transformation. Also, blockchain might not be feasible for multiple reasons, such as existing government, business, and legal agreements and laws, exposure, global reputation, bureaucracy, and partnerships. Therefore, it is important to select the right scope so that you can deliver success incrementally, albeit with a big dream in mind for transformation.

The scope selection exercise reflects your vision and business outcome expectations. However, given that blockchain touches critical elements of an organization's structure, business model, and ecosystem, it is important to consider the scope of each of these items in the context of your desired short-term and long-term business outcomes.

The success of a blockchain project is determined by the correct selection of scope, so define your minimal viable product (MVP) and minimal viable ecosystem (MVE) with a clear start state of your blockchain project; determine your Specific, Measurable, Achievable, Results-focused, and Time-bound (SMART) end goal; and identify key activities that must be performed to pinpoint the following items:

- Vulnerabilities and inefficiencies to identify disruptive business use cases
- Business network participants and ecosystem readiness
- Business model and differentiation needed to compete
- Governance plan and policy for cooperation and trust
- Operational plan, including costs and responsibilities
- Technology and vendor selection

MOTIVATION

The right incentive plan drives motivation to establish the correct behavior, trust, and cooperation in any business network involving consumers and partners. A blockchain network includes both founders of the network and participants. However, because of the nature of the distributed organizations and the decentralized ecosystem that is ready for shared gain and shared pain, it is important to develop an appropriate incentive structure so that everyone is motivated and acts as a trusted partner in the network. Bad actors in a network can jeopardize your ability to achieve your goals within the planned time, costs, and resources conditions.

Incentives in blockchain business networks are not monetary, but might be instead visibility, access, share, and exchange rights. For example, a regulator might want access to and visibility of transactions for compliance purpose, a nonfounding member might want to participate and share its assets for exchange or return value in a network, and a founding member such as a government agency might want specific rights for a business policy or transaction while maintaining trust and transparency.

A token can be issued as an incentive to grow transactions, assets exchange, or the value of transactions in a network. Tokens represent equity or rewards in the systems, and the value of those rewards grow if everyone is performing at an expected or higher level. These tokens are used in managing the loyalty points in retail or consumer businesses, carbon credits in energy trading, credit scores in a financial system, course or merit certification in an educational system, or even a brand or a social image in a reputation system.

To drive sustained motivation in a blockchain network, you must evaluate the following aspects:

- Who brings which data, knowledge, or assets to the network?
- What is the value of their contributions to the network?
- What do they expect in return?
- What will keep them motivated to be trusted participants?
- What incentives you can offer for short-term versus long-term engagement?
- What policies can enable automated incentive allocation?

GOVERNANCE

A good business depends on having a good governance structure and a team of trusted partners. The success and failure of a business entirely depends on its ability to develop an ecosystem that is properly governed and incentivized.

Governance is the most critical and compulsory requirement for a blockchain project's success because it maintains a decentralized property with self-executable business and legal contracts that are embodied in the transactions as smart contracts. Although this approach drives automation, speed, and efficiency in a business network, it is critical to understand how the smart contracts are developed and managed as part of the governance structure. In unforeseeable situations, when you have trusted and motivated partners in a network, consensus building becomes much easier and occurs much faster.

The risk in a blockchain project is directly proportional to the governance complexity that drives increased uncertainty, delays, and costs. The public blockchain networks have higher risks than their private, permissioned, or hybrid counterparts due to the difficulty in governance efficacy. Although some use cases are perfect for public blockchain, others are not. Unless you plan carefully, having an open, public, and decentralized governance structure might not be feasible for many of your enterprise use cases because of privacy, compliance, and regulatory requirements. Because many industries' regulators are investigating blockchain technology implications for their compliance requirements and addressing them, your network must adhere to the existing compliance policies.

A governance structure in a blockchain network can include multiple levels of workgroups that should have a dedicated focus to address the following specific concerns:

- The disruptive nature of the envisioned business model and its impact on participants
- The roles and accountability of participants
- Decision rights
- Shared incentives and disincentives
- Intellectual property rights and liabilities
- Existing regulatory and compliance policies and awareness of future changes
- Technical design and architecture

TECHNOLOGY

Technology concerns are not the primary inhibitors of the adoption of blockchain. Indeed, many organizations, including IBM, have made deliberate efforts to make blockchain ready for enterprise usage by effectively addressing (or being in the process of addressing) implementation, deployment, integration, and operation concerns.

Many businesses might be overwhelmed by the technical challenges regarding privacy, scale, or throughput, such as the number of transactions, interoperability, consensus, contract verification, tools, support, and quantum computing threats. However, many of these concerns have already been addressed by many vendors in various implementations of blockchain technologies.

Permissioned and private blockchains can address the privacy concerns by maintaining the anonymity of a participant while ensuring the validation of a transaction from an authorized participant or by using obfuscation technology to restrict the exposure of private information. In public blockchain implementation, businesses can choose to implement off-chain execution—a practice in which they keep only transactional information recorded on the public ledger, while simultaneously maintaining a shadow ledger to keep identity information private.

The scalability or throughput of the blockchain network primarily depends on the levels of security and cryptography that are applied, as well as the efficiency of the consensus algorithm. If you loosen the security strength, the throughput increases. The proof-of-work module is the primary compute- and time-intensive task that drives the throughput, and many public blockchain implementations for cryptocurrency have single-digit transactions that are validated and recorded per second. By comparison, a robust, enterprise-ready, and permissioned blockchain like Hyperledger is ready to serve more than a thousand transactions per second without compromising any security.

Also, you can run multiple channels in a parallel peer-to-peer scheme. This model addresses throughput concerns and enables blockchain readiness for many enterprise use cases.

Interoperability is another concern, given the existence of different implementations of blockchain technologies, such as Ethereum, Hyperledger, R3's Corda, and Ripple. Although business applications and networks are built on different blockchain bases, eventually they must interoperate in the broader economy. As an analogy, think about how we started with private and closed intranets, which were then called upon to interoperate on the Internet. In the blockchain world, standards and technology groups are already working to address these types of concerns.

Consensus mechanisms and corresponding algorithms are quite advanced in the current technology implementations. For example, Hyperledger addresses fault tolerance and resilience concerns by providing a modular foundation where peers are divided into separate groups that are based on their roles and smart contracts are tailored and run. Contract verifications are fairly managed by emerging smart contract programming languages. Tools, deployment, and operations support is provided by many vendors and open source communities.

To some extent, quantum computing poses a threat to blockchain security because quantum computers can hack any traditional system's cryptography. Nevertheless, post-quantum cryptography, such as lattice cryptography techniques, is available to address quantum computing threats.

Although many technical challenges can be addressed with public, private, permissioned, or hybrid blockchain models, you should be able to clearly identify the following items in your environment:

- The architectural needs of your business use case—that is, whether you use a public, private, permissioned, or hybrid blockchain network
- Open and standard technologies requirements

- Privacy requirements
- Scalability and throughput needs
- Integration capability with existing systems and applications
- End-to-end support for implementation, deployment, and operations
- Interoperability needs

CHAPTER SUMMARY

This chapter covered blockchain technology's disruptive elements that drive transformation across traditional organizational structures, business models, and ecosystems. These characteristics fundamentally open endless opportunities in many industries to innovate and challenge the status quo. The primary challenges for a blockchain project's success are specific to the scope, motivation, and governance rather than to the technology.

REFERENCES

1. Crowe's Financial Cost of Fraud 2018 Report. www.crowe.com/uk/croweuk/insights/financial-cost-of-fraud-2018

2. Gartner, 2018 Worldwide Cybersecurity Forecast Report. www.gartner.com/en/newsroom/press-releases/2018-08-15-gartner-forecasts-worldwide-information-security-spending-to-exceed-124-billion-in-2019

3. Statista, Report: Size of the Cyber Security Market Worldwide, from 2017 to 2022. www.statista.com/statistics/595182/worldwide-security-as-a-service-market-size/

4. International Association for Contract and Commercial Management Report. blog.iaccm.com/commitment-matters-tim-cummins-blog/the-cost-of-a-contract

5. Statista, Report: Size of the Legal Services Market Worldwide from 2013 to 2021. www.statista.com/statistics/605125/size-of-the-global-legal-services-market/

6. Gartner, Forecast: Blockchain Business Value, Worldwide, 2017–2030. www.gartner.com/doc/3627117/forecast-blockchain-business-value-worldwide

7. Michael Burgi, "What's Being Done to Rein in $7 Billion in Ad Fraud," *Adweek*, February 21, 2016.

8. Lucy Handley, "Billions of Digital Marketing Dollars Are Being Wasted as Online Adverts Miss Their Intended Targets: Research," CNBC, December 20, 2016.

3

UNDERSTANDING THE TECHNOLOGY LANDSCAPE

Open technology architecture, economic viability, and longevity of the blockchain network should be some of the primary design criteria.
—Nitin Gaur

Blockchain has tremendous potential and is much more than the sum of its core components. Enterprise blockchain provides a design avenue in which transaction data, value, and state are inherently close to the business logic, and the security of the execution of business transactions is validated by a secure community process, enabling a foundation of trust and the robust processing of transactions. There are certainly virtues to using a blockchain as a technology alternative that is permissioned and conforms to all the regulatory platforms that have evolved over time. Indeed, blockchain promises to solve long-standing industry concerns, such as modernizing the financial and trade system and speeding up securities and trade settlements. The goal is meaningful application of technology to move goods and money seamlessly with full systemic transparency, trust, and accountability of participants, all without an intermediary, and faster and at much lower cost.

BLOCKCHAIN: A TECHNICAL PERSPECTIVE

As described in Chapter 2, blockchain technologies are viewed as a disruptive force for existing industries such as healthcare, supply chains, trade logistics, financial systems, and market infrastructure, and promise to fundamentally change the way that these industries operate. Nevertheless, some thorny challenges related to enterprise adoption must be addressed before you can adopt blockchain:

- Blockchain currently lacks generally accepted definitions and standards. Standards bodies and ISO (International Organization for Standardization) initiatives, such as TC307, are currently attempting to standardize the taxonomy, terminology, and other standards for blockchain. Such standards are essential to widespread adoption of blockchain.

- To use blockchain in their production systems, industries must address the enterprise challenges of transaction audibility, visibility, and integration into existing business functions.

- Blockchain is a cryptographic database technology that was popularized by its association with cybercurrency (for example, Bitcoin and Altcoin). However, the technology itself has the potential to change the world. Blockchain technology solves the issue of time and trust, and provides a platform to eliminate middlemen (disintermediation) regardless of the industry.

- Blockchain-backed business models are emerging that aim to change how industries operate by using co-creation schemes and changing the dynamic of ecosystems. These business models, which are based on digital trust, digital assets, digital (trust) equity, cross-ledger and cross-network transactions, and digital identity, aim to establish blockchain-powered business networks that are trusted and secure, facilitating a new type of interaction that can lead to new business models.

THE FOUR BUILDING BLOCKS

At a basic level, any proposed blockchain solution includes four building blocks: (1) a distributed (or shared) ledger; (2) cryptographic protocols; (3) consensus vehicles (trust system); and (4) chaincode, smart contracts, and business rules (Figure 3.1). These four building blocks collectively form the blockchain technology components, and they have independently existed for decades. Except for evolutionary changes in each of these technology domains, their core principles are understood and accepted.

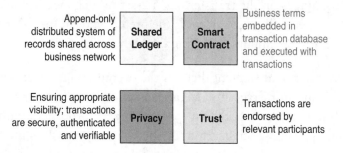

Figure 3.1 The building blocks of blockchain.

Distributed (or Shared) Ledger

Distributed ledgers maintain the record of asset ownership. They are essential to achieve transactional finality. They ensure that the distributed transaction record cannot be changed, and they accept only appended records. Although the intended design of public or permissionless blockchain is to ensure visibility, an enterprise blockchain must account for regulations regarding the privacy of consumer data, and the exposure of business information to competitors.

Cryptographic Protocols

"Cryptography is about constructing and analyzing protocols that prevent third parties or the public from reading private messages."[1] Cryptography enables various systemic attributes of blockchain security, such as transport security, hashing functions, and data and packet encryption. Cryptography also ensures authentication and verifiable transactions.

Cryptography focuses on computational hardness to make cryptography more difficult to break by any adversarial process in the distributed system. Cryptographic protocols work with the consensus or trust systems of a blockchain network. The cryptographic considerations change when they are used in a permissioned ledger network.

Consensus Vehicles (Trust System)

Consensus is essentially a group decision-making process that aids in achieving transaction finality. It is the core of blockchain-powered networks, and it works with the other three components to ensure that the network agrees on the transfer of an asset or a change in the distributed ledger. In general, *trust system* is the preferred term for this component, because not all validation is done through the consensus system.

This foundational element dictates the overall design of and investment in a blockchain infrastructure. Many new and innovative approaches to the trust system in the blockchain space have been proposed, with these variants offering specialization for specific use cases. It is the trust model that makes blockchains effective and delivers the staples of blockchain technology—namely, trust, security, transactionality, trade, and ownership. The trust system is the primary driver of the transaction system that blockchains replace. If *only* trade and ownership were addressed by distributed or shared ledgers, then the plurality might be addressed with an array of database solutions.

Consensus systems directly impact computational costs and the investment required for blockchain-based systems, so you must account for this cost when you are doing system design. Acceptable consensus models are emerging that provide value generation capability to the blockchain-powered networks.

Chaincode, Smart Contracts, and Business Rules

Smart contracts, also known as chaincode, are essentially codified business rules that govern the movement of assets between participants in a network. Chaincode aids in verification validation, and it provides the consensus mechanism that is used for transaction finality.

Blockchains can run code. Although the first blockchains were designed to perform a small set of simple operations (transactions of a digital asset-like token), techniques have since been developed to enable blockchains to perform more complex operations that are defined in full-fledged programming languages. Because these programs are run on a blockchain, they have unique characteristics compared to other types of software, such as business terms that are embedded in a transaction database and run by transactions. This kind of rules component is needed by any business to define the flow of the value and state of a transaction.

WHY BLOCKCHAIN?

So why blockchain? And why now? What makes this technology so special that it has attracted massive investment and forced the likes of supply chains, trade logistics, and the finance industry to rethink their business models under the guise of disruption? The answer likely lies in the Bitcoin blockchain system, which possibly is the only initial functional evidence of a peer-to-peer permissionless network. Although the Bitcoin blockchain system cannot be directly adopted into an enterprise model, much can be learned from it and then applied to a successful blockchain for enterprise.

Bitcoin has gained notoriety for being a radical and unregulated rogue (cyber) currency—a reputation that has prompted some regulated entities to distance themselves from the concept. However, many businesses see the virtues of using blockchain as a technology alternative that is permissioned and conforms to all the regulatory platforms that have evolved over time. Such an approach holds promise as a means to solve long-standing industry concerns, such as modernizing the financial and trade system and speeding up securities and trade settlement. The goal is meaningful application of technology to move goods and money seamlessly with full systemic transparency, trust, and accountability of participants, all without an intermediary, at a faster pace and a much lower cost.

Although the blockchain industry sees a clear separation between the enterprise world and the crypto world, we see a disconnect in understanding the technology trust system that makes a blockchain so attractive. The tenets of Bitcoin are driven by economic incentive (a rewards system for upkeep, longevity, high availability, and system maintenance), cryptography (to

individuals and business entities that participate in a blockchain network. Concepts such as a distributed or decentralized trust, digital identity, self-sovereign identity, consent management, and distributed access control (DACL) are evolving to address the various authentication and authorization needs of a blockchain network.

BLOCKCHAIN FOR ENTERPRISES

As we examine the facets of blockchain technology and their potential benefits to enterprise applications, we realize that the blockchain landscape is fragmented, with many innovative approaches in use to apply this technology to problem solving. This innovation leads to specialization, with each blockchain vendor offering a variant trust system, a different approach to one or more of the blockchain core components (such as the shared ledger, consensus, smart contracts, and cryptography) that addresses a specific business use case. These specialized vendors have defined business use cases that benefit from blockchain's robust trust system, which allows for speed that matches the consumer's expectations of the digital world. The tenets of blockchain—such as decentralized, distributed, global, and permanent code-based programmable assets and records of transaction—can be instrumental in managing such interactions, allowing them to keep up with the speed of the Internet.

As we contemplate the benefits of blockchain technology, we must also consider the adoption of blockchain by enterprises as a mainstream application transaction system. We suggest caution when using blockchain in enterprise application platforms that are burdened by legacy and evolving model-driven designs.

In this section, we attempt to demystify blockchain and outline the challenges that might occur when an enterprise adopts blockchain technology. We also focus on three primary areas that help describe blockchain in the context of an enterprise, as shown in Figure 3.2.

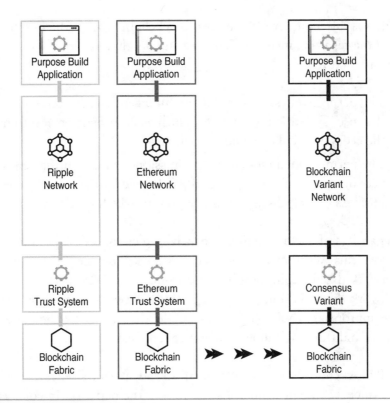

Figure 3.2 Enterprise blockchain.

ENTERPRISE VIEW OF BLOCKCHAIN: TECHNOLOGY AND BUSINESS DOMAIN

When we discuss the technology landscape and enterprise adoption of blockchain, we should draw a distinction between permissioned and permissionless blockchain. Although this distinction is not simple, both types (and their variations) have a few things in common:

- The technology components
- The thematic elements of blockchain technology—that is, trust, transparency, and disintermediation

What is different between the two blockchain types is the business model and the resulting incentive economic model that govern the technology infrastructure:

- The permissionless models rely on an incentivized economic structure that uses systemic crypto assets (such as cryptocurrencies) to maintain the ecosystem balance and participation.
- The permissioned models use permissioned and identified entities and a network economic structure and are defined by the industry consortium business model (discussed in Chapter 4), which relies on compute equity.

Regardless of the distinction, blockchain technology is about networks and ecosystems. Whether you are discussing a peer-to-peer (P2P) permissionless network (like Bitcoin) or a business-to-business (B2B) permissioned network (like We.Trade), the end goal is a network that is supported by the appropriate equitable business model that facilitates the movement of assets and things of value with embedded trust.

P2P blockchains are generally open, so the "permissionless" label is an apt one: No one needs permission to join the network. In contrast, a permissioned blockchain is a network that attracts like-minded businesses and related business ecosystem players who need permission to join the blockchain. The term "consortium" is often used to describe an industry initiative that employs blockchain technology to either transform the industry or combat the disruptive forces of permissionless blockchains. Over time, industries have expanded the classification and the distinction between these two types of blockchains and added blockchain variations because of industry trends and business adoption of various public and consortium blockchain technology platforms and frameworks. New terms have emerged from this process:

- Permissioned public
- Permissioned private
- Federated

- Hybrid
- Permissionless public

Figure 3.3 shows the types of blockchains.

TYPES OF BLOCKCHAINS

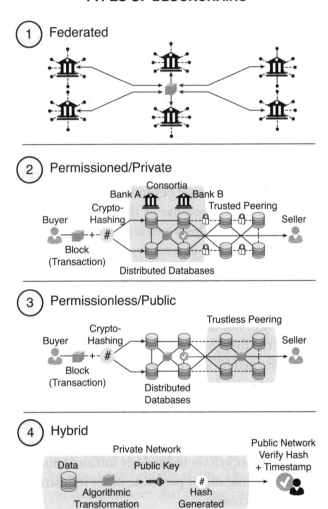

Figure 3.3 Types of blockchains.

the issues for itself, then perhaps it can apply the same acumen to solve the issue for the industry as a whole. This objective leads to determining the network effect—a quest motivated by the revenue objectives of an enterprise, including first market advantage, market leadership, industry transformation, and all the imperatives of the network effects of an ecosystem.

High-level technology considerations include the following issues:

- **Trust system and consensus technology:** Consensus, mining, minting, consortium-specific consensus, cryptographic spectrum, and others.
- **Communication privacy on open networks:** Cryptographic spectrum, encryption, channels, bilateral and multilateral communication, and the inclusion of regulatory and auditory roles.
- **Business integration systems:** Integration into business and enterprise systems, which includes visibility into the stacks of processes.
- **Enterprise system integration:** Meaningful integration with current and legacy systems by using the least disruptive path.

Chain Decision Matrix

Because the implications of this technology can be profound, an enterprise might want to devise a set of enterprise-specific criteria that can be applied to existing or new projects that use blockchain. Because of the versatility of blockchain technology and the current technological evolution curve, enterprises should use the chain decision matrix as a tool to ensure that an enterprise has a structured approach to apply a foundational technology to a business domain. This approach also enables a consistent blockchain infrastructure and trust management system, which proves vital as application-driven chains evolve and demand for enterprise visibility, management, and control grows. Figure 3.4 illustrates the components of such an enterprise blockchain platform.

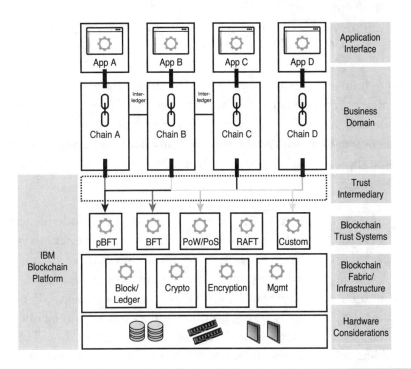

Figure 3.4 An enterprise blockchain platform.

TECHNOLOGY, BUSINESS, AND REGULATORY CONSIDERATIONS FOR BLOCKCHAIN

From a technological perspective, the design goals of adopting blockchain in any enterprise should focus on disrupting the incumbent system as little as possible. One way to achieve this goal is to think about integration with an enterprise system of record, which treats blockchain-driven transaction processing and the enterprise system of record as interfaces for other enterprise applications, such as reporting, business intelligence, and data analytics and regulatory interactions.

A design paradigm should also separate the blockchain technology infrastructure from the business domains that use blockchain technology. This approach establishes blockchain as an enterprise chain infrastructure that is invisible to businesses, while promoting enterprise synergy between the various business-driven chains. It also separates the business domain from the technology that supports it.

Blockchain applications should be provisioned by business domains that use an appropriate trust system that is applicable to the ecosystem for the business domain. Central to any blockchain endeavor is security design and consensus as well as the trust systems that are chosen. The system design should be appropriate to the business model of the blockchain network.

The chosen trust system also dictates the cost of the underlying infrastructure and the compute requirements. The distinctions between the blockchain technology infrastructure, the architecture of the pluggable trust system, the trust intermediaries, and the design allow a business chain to focus on the business and regulatory requirements. Economic viability and longevity of the blockchain network should be one of the primary design criteria. The technology infrastructure should be open, modular, and adaptable to any blockchain variant with specialized offerings, thereby providing manageability.

Enterprise synergy implies driving synergies between the various enterprise blockchains to enable inter-enterprise and intra-enterprise chain (cross-ledger) connections. With this type of model, the transactions cross various trust systems and various aspects of enterprise governance. In addition, control systems are visible to such interactions. The interactions between various business units and external enterprises are important to fractal visibility and are associated with the protection of enterprise data. Invisible enterprise chain infrastructures enable a solid foundation that leads to the evolution of enterprise connectors and the exposure of application programming interfaces (APIs) to enable incumbent systems to be chain-aware. Due to conditional programmable contracts (smart contracts) between the business chains, enterprise synergy flourishes.

Figure 3.5 illustrates the infrastructure elements of an enterprise blockchain.

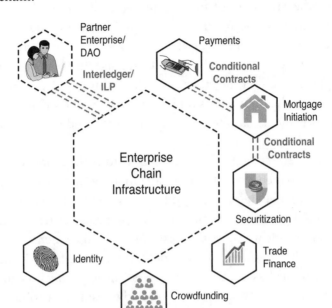

Figure 3.5 Example of an enterprise blockchain infrastructure.

Are enterprises picking the correct use cases to employ blockchain? More importantly, should the consideration of blockchain consumption focus on integration with incumbent transaction systems, or should blockchain technology infrastructures be enterprise-aware? An integrated enterprise needs more than one specialized use case, and it needs to drive enterprise synergy to fully realize the promise of enterprise blockchain. The use cases should be based on fundamental technical tenets and paired with the correct business economic models that support sustainable growth. The technical success of blockchain consumption should initially focus on technology, and enterprises should consider integration with existing enterprise business systems to ease the collective understanding of this technology while establishing a path of least disruption and accelerating enterprise adoption.

ESSENTIAL MATURITY IMPERATIVES FOR ENTERPRISE BLOCKCHAIN

Although the early days of blockchain were all about disruption, education, understanding, investment, and business models, this model now needs to mature and reap the benefits of what industries wanted to achieve: an efficient system with built-in trust that leads to an efficient marketplace based on the efficacy of the technology application. In this section, we go back to basics and focus on the fundamentals of time and trust and the blockchain tenets of trade, trust, and ownership.

Our many client engagements have led us to realize that we still must focus on fundamentals to truly engage in a digital transaction system that includes verifiable digital identity, tokenization of assets (into digital assets), and digital fiat (another digital asset as a settlement vehicle). This focus ensures that we cover the bases of societal elements, such as verifiable claims, nonrepudiation, defining and verifying ownership, and mapping physical assets to digital assets (through tokenization). Moreover, it ensures that the governance system is the result of a robust system design that prevents wrongdoing and fraud and provides confidence that the resulting economic and financial system is ready for the digital age.

Essential elements for enterprise blockchain maturity include the following:

- **Digital identity** as a foundation technology to ensure the trade and ownership tenets of the blockchain system. We need digital identity to assign ownership to a digital asset.
- **Digital fiat** to address the last-mile issue of settlement for every financial transaction and every financial services use case. Money of fiat as a settlement instrument must be digitized to keep pace with the digital transaction network.
- **Asset tokenization** to ensure that digital manifestations reflect real-world assets. A technological platform must ensure that the assets

are digitized, are unique in a system, cannot be replicated and maintain their integrity to hold value, and preserve transfer value.

- **Security design of the blockchain system** to address nonrepudiation, privacy, confidentiality, and verifiability of claims with consent-driven models.

- **Business of blockchain business models** to ensure that regulated and enterprise systems can find the correct business model to advance the agenda of blockchain-based business networks.

- A **governance model**, which may range from a self-governance network to a consortium-defined semi-autonomous governance structure. Again, you must find the correct governance model necessary to progress the agenda of blockchain-based business networks.

Figure 3.6 depicts the essential elements of an enterprise blockchain.

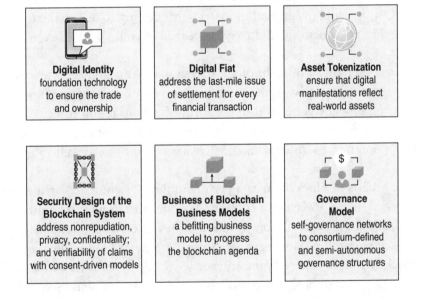

Figure 3.6 Essential elements of an enterprise blockchain.

TOKEN REVOLUTION

ASSET TOKENIZATION: ESSENTIAL TO POWERING THE NEXT-GENERATION DIGITAL "INSTANCE" ECONOMY

One of the core value propositions of a blockchain-powered network is the resulting co-creation elements, such as the digital transaction system and the value-driven ecosystem and marketplace. Asset tokenization is essential to powering the next-generation digital economy and paving the way for new business models that are built on the "instance economy." To explore this topic, let us begin with some background.

Earlier, we discussed the challenges of the permissionless world, which does not adhere to any conventions and forges ahead with many innovations that are bound to disrupt many industries. Those changes may be advanced either through new business designs (e.g., initial coin offerings [ICOs]) or by conventional industries attempting to adopt the technology to either transform the industry or beat or keep up with disruption.

This combination of technology-driven platforms and the use cases that depend on them rely on the manifestation of value. Digitization—whether it is systemically generated in the form of a transaction utility coin or a layer-two token that relies on the underlying coin for its value—is nothing but a notation of an instrument that has a real or perceived value.

The genesis of blockchain as a permissionless system relied on a technology-based systemic governance composed of incentives and mechanisms of coordination. This systemic governance has its own set of challenges when it is used in enterprise business networks that attempt to use the tenets of blockchain technology. In the enterprise world, which is regulated and relies on permissioned blockchain models, the checks-and-balances system is complicated by transactions between competing entities that use regulated data and have a fiduciary responsibility. Such permissioned models cannot account for the tangible or systemically generated incentives (crypto-assets) or have network-wide mechanisms of coordination due to privacy and confidentiality issues. Figure 3.7 provides a view of the various types of blockchain and industry use cases.

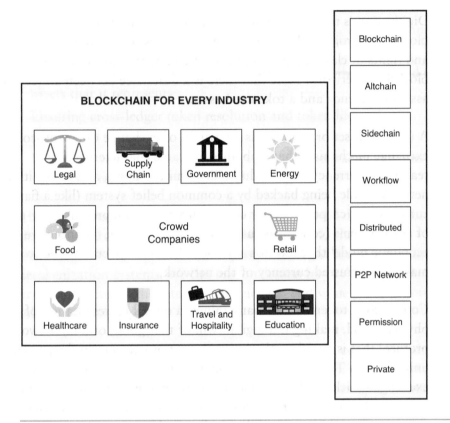

Figure 3.7 Types of blockchain and industry use cases.

INTRODUCTION TO TOKENIZATION: UNDERSTANDING THE TOKEN REVOLUTION

Blockchain technology lays the foundation for a trusted digital transactional network that, as a disintermediated platform, fuels the growth of marketplaces and secondary markets due to new synergies and co-creation that come from new digital interactions and value-exchange mechanisms. Although blockchain itself provides the technology constructs to facilitate exchange, ownership, and trust in the network, it is in the digitization

- Tokenized securities
- Security tokens
- Utility tokens
- Collateralized and decentralized tokens
- Non-collateralized and decentralized tokens
- Collateralized and centralized tokens
- Initial coin offering (ICO)
- Security token offering (STO)

VARIOUS INDUSTRY DEFINITIONS

Here are some definitions of tokenization from industry sources:

> This is where stable coins come in. Stable coins are price-stable cryptocurrencies, meaning the market price of a stable coin is pegged to another stable asset, like the US dollar.[2]

> Preston Byrne: A stable coin claims to be an asset that prices itself, rather than an asset that is priced by supply and demand.[2]

> In their most simplistic form, stable coins are simply cryptocurrencies with stable prices measured in fiat currency.[3]

> Types of stable coins: fiat collateralized, crypto collateralized, non-collateralized, collateralized decentralized, collateralized centralized, pegged, and so on.[3]

> Tokenization is a method that converts rights to an asset into a digital token.[4]

> Tokenization is the process of converting rights to an asset into a digital token on a blockchain. There is great interest by financial intermediaries and technologists around the world in figuring out how to move real-world assets onto blockchains to gain the advantages of Bitcoin while keeping the characteristics of the asset.[5]

The varying industries (crypto and financial services and analyst communities) have varying points of view and definitions. This diversity makes it incredibility difficult to define concepts like technology or digital assets or traditional and conventional risk models.

Now that we have explored the token revolution and drawn a distinction between (crypto) assets and currency, let us explore the token valuation models and why they are important.

Token Valuation Models and the Instance Economy

Although an (crypto) asset or currency derives its value as a medium of exchange within a shared common belief system of a network (often confined to that network), tokens might have complex and fragmented valuation models. Many coins (started by ICOs and STOs) that aspire to morph into their own crypto assets, either as utility or security tokens, rely on the community to develop and recognize value. In contrast, many other tokens are only digital representations of the assets that they represent.

Assets today, such as stocks, bonds, securities, mortgages, and mortgage-backed securities, are difficult to transfer or subdivide physically, so buyers and sellers instead trade paper (or digital records) that represents these assets. The issue with paper (or digital records) and their accompanying complex legal agreements is that they are cumbersome and pose a challenge to transference and tracking, leading to opacity, fraud, opportunity, and transaction costs. One solution is to switch to a digital system that uses digital assets, such as tokenized assets on a blockchain network, but linked to an asset.

It might be prudent for us to classify these token valuations by either industry type (such as nonfinancial, supply chain, or financial services) or asset type (dematerialized, virtual, real asset, and others). Such a classification is necessary to establish a trail of governance with checks and balances and to represent some industry-recognized valuation systems. With this approach, it might seem as if all that we are achieving from tokenizing assets on blockchain networks is mimicking or creating a digital twin of current value networks, and that a fiat currency, although it addresses the duality of a transaction, can be replaced by a cryptocurrency (including digital fiat). In reality, the promise of blockchain-based business networks is not just about digitization and solving the inefficiencies of time and trust, but also about creating new business models and co-creation that capitalizes on the synergies of the network participants.

Thus, we see the introduction of the instance economy and secondary markets that are fueled by the instances of an asset. Tokenization of assets can lead to creation of a business model that fuels fractional ownership or the ability to own an instance of a large asset. Fractional ownership opens a market to participation from entities that were prevented from participating due to high capital requirements or the opacity of the value transfer systems. Furthermore, fractional ownership opens up a new range of asset classes and asset types, unlocking the economic value of capital that could not previously be accessed as investment opportunities.

We use the term *instance economy* because this type of economy fuels the tokenization of assets, which leads to the ownership of an instance of an asset class. This approach creates markets and secondary markets of value.

Although blockchain provides the technology constructs to facilitate exchange, ownership, and trust in the network, it is in the digitization of value elements that asset tokenization is truly essential. Tokenization is the process of converting the assets and rights or claims to an asset into a digital representation, or token, in a blockchain network. The distinction between cryptocurrency and tokenized assets is an important construct for understanding the exchange vehicles, valuation models, and fungibility across various value networks that are emerging. These networks pose challenges related to technical interoperability and equitable swaps. Tokenization of assets can lead to the creation of a business model that fuels fractional ownership or the ability to own an instance of a large asset. The promised asset tokenization within blockchain-based business networks depends on digitization and solving the inefficiencies of time and trust, and it creates new business models and co-creation from the synergies of the network participants.

Understanding Digital Asset (Token) Fungibility: Opportunities and Challenges Related to Token Valuation and Blockchain Ecosystems

Since the early conversations about crypto assets and blockchain, there has been a significant change in attitudes toward crypto assets and the industry's willingness to work toward solving the issues regarding the trade, payment, and movement of (digital) goods and money. Some of the industry's focus has centered on the economic viability of solutions, business models, and governance, and the fundamental tenets of blockchain and its correct use in use cases, such as the following ones:

- The payments landscape: Retail, wholesale, interbank, and cross-border issues.
- The relevance to GPI Phase 3 and blockchain's role regarding Nostros Vostro.
- Stable coin and digital fiat: Payment innovation, payment velocity, and emerging business models.
- Innovation in B2B products, such as accounts payable, accounts receivable, and B2B money transfers.

Although we are building a value network that can transfer value with embedded trust and transparency, in many cases the value is created by using the principles of crypto economic models (mining, minting, or simply induced value) or, in the case of permissioned networks, by introducing asset tokenization. You should understand the primary drivers of value in a blockchain network, which inform the understanding of the core tenets used to evaluate the economic value of blockchain entities. The drivers of valuation include the following possibilities:

- Tokens that are driven by crypto economic models, which are themselves driven by supply and demand and the utility of the network.
- Non-fungible tokens (NFTs) that have an intrinsic value, such as identity, diplomas, and healthcare records. Such tokens are simple

proof-validations of the existence, authenticity, and ownership of digital assets.

- Fungible tokens that are valued by the total of economic activity in the network (cryptocurrency); their utility (smart contracts and transaction network processing); their assigned values, as in stable coins and security tokens; and so on.

At this point, we must define and understand tokenized value. Many different token types and classifications exist, all of which share one thing in common: They represent and digitize value.

DEFINING FUNGIBILITY

In economics, *fungibility* is "the property of a good or a commodity whose individual units are essentially interchangeable."[6] That definition has implications for the blockchain world, owing to its reliance on tokens and their economic models. In this section, we explore two fundamentals of token-based systems:

- The token evaluation model
- Token fungibility and asset exchange mechanisms

The Token Evaluation Model

The token evaluation model determines the value of a systemic asset. Put simply, if we choose to engage in economic activity such as transaction processing and use the asset as a currency, or if we use tokens as a utility or security, we must know what the asset or token is worth!

Considerations for evaluating the economic values of blockchain companies include the following:

- **Business solutions:**
  - **Problem domains:** What is the business problem that we are solving? What is the industry landscape? What is our evolution through innovation?

- **Addressable markets:** What is the overall cost of problem domains? For example, what is the cost of the problem itself or industry subsegments?

- **The regulatory and compliance landscape:** The regulatory landscape can help or impede the adoption of new technology-led business models.

- **Competitive frameworks and alternatives:** How are the other framework entities trying to solve the issue with or without DLT or blockchain?

- Technology design and architecture:

  - **Consensus design:** This approach leads to trust systems and the economic viability of the blockchain network.

  - **Blockchain tenets:** Shared ledgers, crypto elements, smart contracts, and security elements are foundational concepts.

  - **Blockchain deployment infrastructure:** The cloud, geo-specific deployment, technical talent (or access to it), service level agreements (SLAs), and other components must be defined for the network.

- Monetization strategies:

  - **Token-based models:** Operation fees are used to write to the blockchain-powered business network's distributed database.

  - **Tokens as a medium of exchange:** Participating entities lend or sell tokens as a step-through currency.

  - **Asset-pair trading:** This practice monetizes margins.

  - **Commercialization of the protocol:** Technology services include the cloud and software, lab, and consulting services.

The Power of Networks

We can extrapolate the power of networks and the exponential power of co-creation models to create new business models and produce economic value.

and businesses as a means to solve current problems and pave the way for new business models (enterprise and subsequent industry focus). As the industry and enterprises realize the potential of blockchain technology and reimagine today's business networks, which are laden with archaic processes, paper- and document-driven processes, and systemic costs, they must also address long-term considerations related to adopting the blockchain-powered business network.

To use blockchain effectively, you must consider other mechanics of the business network:

- **Choice matrix of consensus models:** The industry must develop a choice matrix for consensus models that define the trust system, collusion vector, associated computation costs, and infrastructure investment necessary to support the trust system that defines the business network.

- **Systemic industry governance:** Technology and industry-specific governance is necessary for the systemic digital assets, industry-specific requirements, and business systems that govern the movement, whether permanent or temporary, of digital or tokenized assets within a specific ecosystem. Essentially, such governance defines which entities can do what, who is responsible, and who investigates if a system anomaly arises. These questions, which are industry-specific concerns, must be codified in system design and network initialization.

- **Asset tokenization, control, and governance:** Industry-specific elements are needed to govern asset issuance, collateralization, proof of ownership and existence, and audit requirements so as to ensure the integrity of the real assets in the system. The idea is to weave checks and balances into the system that control supply and demand and establish an audit trail to maintain systemic trust in the business network.

- **Decentralized authority framework:** The notion of decentralized control and authority is tightly linked with the trust system. Of course, in a decentralized system, the notion of authority does not work well. The focus of this design principle, therefore, is on governance, culpability, and regulations.

- **Decentralization and security considerations:** Decentralization and distributed ledgers have various trust advantages, such as a transparency, immutability, and network-wide transaction processing. Although these advantages lend themselves to the overall trust framework, they can also create enterprise challenges concerning distributed data, as well as business insights that can provide a competitive advantage to some participants and a disadvantage to others. The security design imperative is to factor in enterprise security while addressing the new security challenges imposed by a shared business network. Cybersecurity risks and vulnerabilities are high-focus areas.

Business networks are industry-, industry segment–, and asset-specific networks, which implies that no single dominant blockchain controls all other blockchains, and that many blockchain business networks exist. A blockchain network can focus on a plurality of business domains, such as mortgages, payments, exchanges, and clearing and settling specific asset types. In enterprise blockchain, these projects take place within a centralized (in a decentralized context and application design patterns) network that is a consensus consortium between like-minded business entities. This assumption is based on many practical factors:

- **Industry-, segment-, and asset-specific business language:** This language defines the smart contract, asset definition, and control and governance of smart contracts as a proxy business representation.
- **Industry-specific asset control:** This factor defines governance, management, and valuation (for asset exchange, asset fungibility, and others) of digital (representation or) tokenization of assets.
- **Industry- and region-specific regulation:** Most business networks are both industry- and region-specific in their scope. In regulated industries, a business network is regulated separately in terms of the burden of adherence, compliance, and related costs that are shared in the business network.
- **Industry-specific business functions:** Most industries have their own measurements, standards, and statistics that represent performance indicators, such as analytics and market data.

models of a regulator are different from the cost models of the primary beneficiary of the blockchain-powered business network.

- **Shared business model—shared costs and shared benefits:** Because a blockchain-based business network is a network and ecosystem, it features shared business processes instead of flattened business processes. A blockchain-powered business network has specific business advantages, such as reduced risk, a reliable and predictable transaction network, and a reduced cost of compliance, which collectively lead to good ROI ratios.

However, shared business interest leads to other operational considerations, such as data sharing and data ownership as entities join and leave the network. The regulations around data ownership may also change from time to time, along with industry requirements regarding the durability of data. The shared cost of infrastructure, compliance, and efficiencies due to flattened business processes on a blockchain network are clear advantages of this approach, but these efficiencies can be achieved only with a sustainable structure of a business network and the correct economic models.

BLOCKCHAIN PROJECT SUSTAINABILITY

Many design areas—such as business models, technology design, the trust system choice matrix, devising and employing a governance structure, and continual system analysis—are paths to ensure early success with blockchain project deployment and long-term sustainability. The idea is to design a robust, extensible, and organic system that can grow with the changing demands of a business ecosystem, and not be locked into a technology with limited flexibility.

Factors such as scale, security, data visibility, and network extensibility can be exploited to create a sustainable business network. After the network evolves and grows, there is no turning back regarding systemic issues, such as a trust models, data visibility, and competitive advantage while using the network for the shared costs of doing business. Maintaining a substantive focus on sustainability is a complex and paradoxical quest: It promotes open collaborative innovation while locking down some of the constructs, such as consensus or trust systems, and governance systems that govern the assets, smart contracts, and overall interaction in a multiparty transaction network.

As we debate the merits of signing transactions versus mining transactions to establish trust in the network, note that a blockchain-powered business network is limited by the limits of the current business network as it evolves. This is not a technology problem, but rather a business ambition issue. If the system design of the business network is not aligned well with the tenets of blockchain (trade, trust, ownership, and transactionality in a multiparty scenario), the greatest strengths of blockchain might become its greatest weakness, and the business network might not fully realize the promise of blockchain networks. Wise choices for factors such as scale, security, data visibility, and network extensibility, however, can lead to a sustainable business network.

CHAPTER SUMMARY

This chapter discussed the overall blockchain technology landscape and addressed the trust divide between an enterprise (permissioned) blockchain and a public (permissionless) blockchain. It is vital to understand the technology underpinnings of the trust systems, which lay the foundation for trustless interactions between various participants within a network. Enterprise blockchain design and enterprise integration will inevitably impact the cost of the solution deployment and the longevity of the application, so economic incentives are a vital component of any blockchain network. This distinction is vital for the valuation of crypto assets and to ensure the continued and sustained growth of a blockchain-powered business network.

finality. It also can dramatically change the design of the existing processes inside of an enterprise.

Implementation of blockchain for targeted use cases that encompass transaction processing is intended to reduce operational costs and open up new business opportunities that rely on the "network effect" of bringing multiple participants under the same blockchain umbrella. Potential benefits from such cooperation include sharing of the costs of risk profiling and analysis and the approval process, mitigation of systemic risk, and rewards for participating enterprises. With many blockchains, the notion of cost optimization is due to shared costs of many components, which is fundamentally enabled by flattening the existing business process at the network level. In this way, participants broaden their scope, unlock individual enterprise business processes, and open flattened network-wide business processing. This mind-set, however, requires a radical shift in planning and devising a business model.

To give structure to this planning paradigm, we need a device methodology. The prescribed methodology proposes a four-step process that enables an enterprise to channel its resources judiciously, mitigate risk at every level, and ensure that the work product at every step of the way can be functionally applied to a collective decision-making process. The four steps are as follows:

1. Identify an appropriate use case.
2. Devise a business blueprint by distilling the existing business process.
3. Map the business blueprint to technology tenets—that is, devise a technology blueprint.
4. Ensure enterprise integration with (legacy) enterprise systems.

The core and fundamental thinking behind this approach is to enable a business-driven focus and ensure that the correct acumen is applied to the right set of key performance indicators (KPIs) to measure the success of the project and achieve the intended results. We take a singular use case that has impacts on the industry and enterprise, and we apply business and technology acumen to the problem domain. The use-case selection process tests the resolve and commitment of LOB owners. The result is a well-thought-out business architecture and technology blueprint with requirements for compliance, audit, and enterprise integration.

Let us go into detail into each of these steps, which are summarized visually in Figure 4.1.

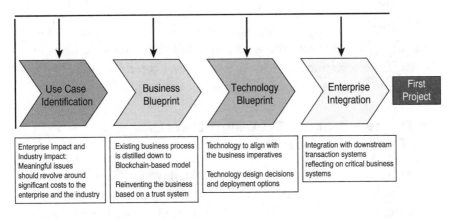

Figure 4.1 Path to blockchain enterprise adoption.

1. IDENTIFY AN APPROPRIATE USE CASE

We should expend a significant amount of time and effort at this stage to ensure that the use case that we pick has two sets of characteristics:

- **Enterprise impact:** The use case that is destined for blockchain adoption after it passes the blockchain tenets tests (trade, trust, ownership, and transactionality) addresses enterprise time and trust issues, which results in significant cost savings, and addresses time and trust imperatives that manifest as redundant systems and processes. This step helps justify costs, investment in the blockchain project, and overall ROI—a language that business understands.

- **Industry impact:** Blockchain promises to create a network of value, which implies an interconnected set of networks that help transfer things of value with relative ease and at significantly lower cost due to the implied trust in the system, which eliminates the need for trust intermediaries. Thus, the use case that is picked should address industry-wide issues—that is, the enterprise cohorts should have a similar set of issues. Some examples include capital market interactions between lenders and borrowers, corporate actions, and others.

The Idea

The effort of selecting meaningful issues should revolve around addressing significant costs to enterprise and industry. This rationale helps justify costs if the investment at the enterprise level is *only* to use a "network effect" as industry adopts blockchain as a trust platform.

2. DEVISE A BUSINESS BLUEPRINT: DISTILLING AN EXISTING BUSINESS PROCESS

Next, we apply a design-thinking approach, where the idea is to distill the existing business process into a blockchain-based transaction model. In this step, the idea is to elucidate all aspects of the existing business process, including its compliance requirements and dependencies on external systems. Furthermore, as we progress in this step, the existing business process is distilled down to the blockchain-based model, which espouses characteristics such as provenance, immutability, flat ledgers, and smart contracts that govern the validation and distribution of the ledgers.

This step is important because the work products generated in this stage lead into the technology design and blueprint. This process defines technical elements, such as the block data format, consensus, structure, and governance of (chain code) smart contracts (essentially the design of the interactions between various enterprise entities and external entities in the future, as industry aims for a network effect), as well as the trust and governance models.

The Idea

Blockchain promises to create a network of value that leads to a concept of the business network. Thus, it is important to understand interaction patterns, inefficiencies, and vulnerabilities, and to develop blockchain models to address those factors. After all, we are reinventing the business based on a trust system.

3. MAP THE BUSINESS BLUEPRINT TO TECHNOLOGY TENETS: DEVISING A TECHNOLOGY BLUEPRINT

The work product from devising a business blueprint feeds into the development of a technology blueprint. This plan aids in making the many necessary technology decisions, such as (among others) the choice of the blockchain data model; consensus, audit, and logging requirements; deployment models; transaction requirements; data visibility; and overall systemic security, including authentication and authorization.

This is a progressive step, which implies that the more time and acumen an enterprise expends on earlier steps devising a blockchain technology blueprint, the more likely the exercise is to yield an accurate and precise deployment model. At this stage, critical and long-lasting technology decisions are made, such as the block data format (which is compatible with the downstream system, or it might need transformation for integration), consensus (based on the interactions with both internal and external systems), fractal visibility of data (based on various business interactions and rules), integration with existing security systems, and the technology stack and deployment (cloud, on-premises, or hybrid), which is an operational concern and significant cost consideration.

The Idea

For technology to align with business imperatives, we must ensure that we are making the correct technology and architecture choices to address the business requirements—such as transactions per second (TPS), technical service level agreements (SLAs), enterprise integration, external system integration, and regulatory and compliance requirements—that make blockchain function in an enterprise. These considerations also require technical due diligence to clarify the blockchain project's budget and mitigate its risks.

4. Ensure Enterprise Integration with (Legacy) Enterprise Systems

We also should consider adjunct enterprise systems that require enterprise integration for blockchain applications for operational considerations. The idea is to verify the presence of the key elements of trade, trust, and ownership, and the inherent properties of blockchain, such as immutability, provenance, and consensus. The resulting trust system should ideally help eliminate redundant and duplicative systems and processes. These duplicative systems require the use of significant resources, leading to delayed transaction processing and associated opportunity costs.

Our goal should be to address the fundamental pain point of the existing process, leading to a flat and transparent ledger that aims to address the element of trust and time, produce significant cost savings, and support better client service.

The Idea

Enterprise integration, especially with an adjacent system, is an important consideration and a cost point. It is both a business consideration and a technology consideration due to the presence of downstream transaction systems, which rely on critical business systems. In many cases, the adjacent system integration has a significant cost impact on the blockchain project. Thus, if this integration is not taken into account early in the planning stages, it can impose a sometimes tricky challenge on enterprise adoption.

Business Modeling and Design

A good blockchain network design encompasses various participants with varied interests who are focused on a singularity of assets and things of value at the nucleus of the blockchain-driven business network and ecosystem, which leads to new partnerships and co-creation synergies. Spending adequate time on devising the correct blockchain business model is essential for blockchain business network success and growth. Indeed, an appropriate business design is an important consideration for blockchain projects beyond the proof of concept (POC) phase. This design considers the various candidate blockchain business models: After the list of potential use cases is narrowed and a use case is finally chosen, the next step is defining the business structure to account for business transformation and disruption.

In the previous section, we described a prescriptive approach that starts with appropriate use case identification and defines a business blueprint before engaging in POC experiments and deeper technology-driven exercises, such as mapping the correct technology and making design decisions that lead to economically viable solutions. To date, the blockchain technical community, the entrepreneurial community, and the industry that aspire to transform and protect against disruptive forces have expended much of their energy on technology design, debating the correct technology approach, correct data structure, consensus models, and overall deployment choices. By comparison, less attention has been paid to the overall business design that will be the foundation of the blockchain networks and ecosystems.

Essentially, many industries seem to be looking at blockchain as a technology platform that will either transform the industry (by improving cost-efficiency, compliance costs, transparency, and so on) or disrupt it (through disintermediation, creation of new intermediaries, co-creation models, and so on). In either case, blockchain is a network of participants that form the ecosystem and coordinated decision-making process to achieve transaction finality and to facilitate a platform that fosters co-creation between the network participants. As blockchain networks evolve and grow, and as new participants are added or removed, the dynamics of the network will undoubtedly change, and bilateral and multilateral relationships may emerge. These changes are largely driven by static bilateral or multilateral engagements that are enforced by chaincode or smart contracts.

shared services, legal services, and administration. Likewise, it clearly separates blockchain network business from business and technology operations.

- A well-thought-out business model for blockchain networks provides an important avenue for business continuity, funding and sourcing models, and overall growth that is driven by the economic and financial structure of the business network, which is itself powered by the tenets of blockchain technology.

- A well-crafted business design restores balance and facilitates smooth interactions between the various entities that compete with some network participants, and it justifies the need to cooperate and co-create with some other network participants. The co-creation element of a blockchain network is essential for sustained longevity and growth of the businesses in the blockchain network.

- A blockchain business network also can be a business. A platform that facilitates co-creation and new synergies must be managed and operated with defined SLAs and have a robust governance structure that attracts new participants and sustains the confidence and business benefits enjoyed by its founders and existing participants.

Figure 4.2 illustrates four types of business models for blockchain networks.

Various business models that are being considered for permissioned or industry-specific blockchain networks include the following:

- Joint venture
- Consortium
- NewCo
- Business ecosystem
- Build–own–operate (BOO) or founder-led networks
- Build–own–operate–transfer (BOOT) or founding consortium–led network

Founder-led Network

Single company driving the initial project, then others join the network

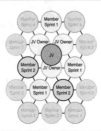

Joint Venture Network

Two or more create a joint venture to govern the initial network

Consortium Network

A consortium as the initial network and governance in a specific industry or sector

Business Ecosystem

A Consortium Network working across multiple industries or sectors

Figure 4.2 Four types of business models for blockchain networks.

Joint Venture

A joint venture (JV) is an entity formed between two or more parties to undertake and operate an economic activity together. In a JV structure, two or more parties agree to create a legal business entity, may fund it with equity contributions and other sources of investment, and share the revenues, operating expenses, and operational control of the enterprise.

- **Advantages:** Ability for companies to gain new expertise, markets, and a disjointed advantage to grow and share a risk model with like-minded businesses.
- **Disadvantages:** The possibility of inequality of skills, investment, and so on, between companies, leading to operational imbalance and difficult decision making.
- **Blockchain technology choices and impact:** A semi-decentralized network that includes some aspects of centralization (the transaction processing can be decentralized). Governance of the business lies with the JV, which can be an impediment for some market players due to perceived competition.

Consortium

A consortium is typically an industry-specific association of two or more organizations with the objective of participating in an industry-specific business or a common activity to achieve a common goal and capitalize on the synergy between industrial players. In a consortium, each participant retains its individual legal status. Collectively, the members may create a consortium governing body to manage the consortium's activities, bylaws, and engagements, and are often joined by various contractual vehicles.

- **Advantages:** Flexible contractual terms that can be altered as the industry evolves. Business advantages of taxation, regulatory adherence, and development of an industry voice for self-governance.
- **Disadvantages:** Issues of liability and nonperformance.

- **Blockchain technology choices and impact:** Semi-decentralized/fully decentralized network. Included are some aspects of centralization, and the transaction processing can be decentralized. Governance can be decentralized by imposing self-governance rules or adopting a consensus mechanism for governance and a flexible technology design because governance structures can evolve. Industry-specific models may evolve, along with singularity regarding products, services, industry norms, and regulatory requirements.

NewCo

NewCo is a generic name for a proposed spin-off from an enterprise, consortium, or subsidiary before a formal name is chosen. A NewCo may be a new legal entity or a combined entity formed by existing entities.

- **Advantages:** The ability for companies to gain new expertise, markets, a disjointed advantage to grow, and limited risk and exposure for the parent company.
- **Disadvantages:** Possibility of a lack of skills, investment, and support structure.
- **Blockchain technology choices and impact:** A semi-decentralized network or, in some cases, a centralized network that disregards the core tenets of blockchain and that uses piecemeal advantages of the technology. This model includes some aspects of centralization, and the transaction processing can be decentralized. Governance of the business lies with the NewCo, which can be an impediment for some market players due to perceived competition.

Business Ecosystem

A typical business ecosystem flourishes by combining a platform-thinking approach with a model that includes the networks of existing organizations; these organizations seek to capitalize on new business opportunities by creating an environment that facilitates co-creation and combines business models to introduce a unique value proposition for the customer. An example is a marketplace that includes suppliers, distributors, customers, competitors, government entities, and adjacent linked industries to deliver a unique value proposition through both cooperating and competing.

- **Advantages:** Flexible contractual terms that can be altered as the industry evolves. Business advantages of taxation, regulatory adherence, and development of an industry voice for self-governance.
- **Disadvantages:** Issue of liability, accountability, likability, and nonperformance.
- **Blockchain technology choices and impact:** Can be designed as a fully decentralized network. Governance of the business ecosystem can be decentralized by imposing self-governance rules or adopting a consensus mechanism for governance. A flexible technology design enables the governance structure to evolve. Operations, SLAs, and overall platform management must have a centralized undertaking.

Build–Own–Operate or Founder-Led Networks

The BOO model is usually adopted by a public–private partnership in which the private entity builds, owns, and operates a structure or a facility, and public entities may provide assistance in the form of tax incentives, licensing and governance, and other supports. These models can vary in the permissioned world, where a founder or an industry leader can build, own, and operate the network and shape the industry to its advantage.

- **Advantages:** The founding entity gets the benefit of established industry leadership and the residual value of the network, including revenue streams and adjacent business models.
- **Disadvantages:** Potential requirement for significant investment in top talent, capital, and enterprise support resources to garner senior executives and internal business ecosystem support.
- **Blockchain technology choices and impact:** A semi-decentralized network or, in some cases, a centralized network, which disregards the

core tenets of blockchain and uses piecemeal advantages of technology. This model includes some aspects of centralization, and transaction processing can be decentralized. Governance of the business lies with network operations that are managed by the founder, which can be an impediment for some market players due to perceived competition.

Build–Own–Operate–Transfer or Founding Consortium–Led Network

BOOT is a type of business structure, rather than a form of financing. In this model, an entity usually receives concessions or funding (either private or public) to design, construct, own, and operate the project, which is either a facility or a business network, for a purpose that is outlined in a series of business and concession contracts. The facility or network is then transferred to a different entity, and the founding entity can use a bidding process to leverage the business value of operating the facility or business network.

- **Advantages:** Development of avenues of investment due to the business value of transfer potential. Flexible models as the industry evolves.

- **Disadvantages:** The blockchain network and adjacent services are the business model itself. This approach can carry high risks due to maturity issues and the adoption of technology and business design.

- **Blockchain technology choices and impact:** A semi-decentralized network or. in some cases. a centralized network, which disregards the core tenets of blockchain and uses piecemeal advantages of technology. This model includes some aspects of centralization, and transaction processing can be decentralized. Governance of the business lies with network operations that are managed by the founder, which can be an impediment for some market players due to perceived competition.

Table 4.1 describes the various types of business models' value matrix for blockchain networks.

Table 4.1 Business Models' Value Matrix for Blockchain Networks

Business Model	Advantages	Disadvantages	Blockchain Technology Choices and Impact
Joint venture	Ability for companies to gain new expertise and new markets; a disjointed advantage to grow and share a risk model with like-minded businesses.	Possible inequality of skills, investment, and others between companies, which leads to operational imbalance and difficult decision making.	A semi-decentralized network that includes some aspects of centralization, with decentralized transaction processing. Governance of the business lies with the joint venture, which can be an impediment for some market players due to perceived competition.
Consortium	Flexible contractual terms that can be altered as the industry evolves. Business advantages of taxation, regulatory adherence, and development of an industry voice for self-governance.	Issues of liability and nonperformance.	Semi-decentralized/fully decentralized network. The model includes some aspects of centralization, and transaction processing can be decentralized. Governance can be decentralized by imposing self-governance rules or adopting a consensus mechanism for governance and a flexible technology design, reflecting the potential for governance structures to evolve. Industry-specific models and singularity regarding products, services, industry norms, and regulatory requirements.
NewCo	The ability for companies to gain new expertise and markets, a disjointed advantage to grow, and limited risk and exposure for the parent company.	Possible lack of skills, investment, and support structure.	A semi-decentralized network or, in some cases, a centralized network, which disregards the core tenets of blockchain and uses piecemeal advantages of technology. The model includes some aspects of centralization, and transaction processing can be decentralized. Governance of the business lies with the NewCo, which can be an impediment for some market players due to perceived competition.

Business Model	Advantages	Disadvantages	Blockchain Technology Choices and Impact
Business ecosystem	Flexible contractual terms that can be altered as the industry evolves. Business advantages of taxation, regulatory adherence, and development of an industry voice for self-governance.	Issue of liability, accountability, likability, and nonperformance.	A fully decentralized network. Governance can be decentralized by imposing self-governance rules or adopting a consensus mechanism for governance. A flexible technology design enables the governance structure to evolve. Operations, SLAs, and overall platform management must have a centralized undertaking.
Build–own–operate (BOO) or founder-led networks	The founding entity gets the benefit of an established industry leadership and the residual value of the network, including revenue streams and adjacent business models.	Might require significant investment in top talent, capital, and enterprise support resources to garner senior executives and internal business ecosystem support.	A semi-decentralized network or, in some cases, a centralized network, which disregards the core tenets of blockchain and uses piecemeal advantages of technology. The model includes some aspects of centralization, and transaction processing can be decentralized. Governance of the business lies with network operations that are managed by the founder, which can be an impediment for some market players due to perceived competition.
Build–own–operate–transfer (BOOT) or founding consortium-led network	Development of avenues of investment due to the business value of transfer potential. Flexible models as the industry evolves.	The blockchain network and adjacent services are the business model itself. Can carry high risks due to maturity issues and the adoption of technology and business design.	A semi-decentralized network or, in some cases, a centralized network, which disregards the core tenets of blockchain and uses piecemeal advantages of technology. Includes some aspects of centralization, and transaction processing can be decentralized. Governance of the business lies with network operations that are managed by the founder, which can be an impediment for some market players due to perceived competition.

CHAPTER SUMMARY

When defining the path to blockchain enterprise adoption, key considerations are maintaining a narrow focus on a singular use case and distilling the existing business into a blockchain paradigm, which implies the development of both business and technology models. Specifically, we must identify a singular use case that has both industry and enterprise impacts and apply business and technology acumen to the problem domain. The result should be a well-thought-out business architecture and technology blueprint, along with requirements for compliance, audit, and enterprise integration. The point of this exercise is to devote your time and energy, in combination with the right business domain expertise and blockchain technology expertise, to derive an adoption model that unearths and solves hurdles, challenges, and problematic factors affecting the costs and economic viability of the proposed blockchain solution. The resulting artifacts and collateral of the blockchain garage engagement are instrumental in socialization and in providing a blueprint for a business seeking executive sponsorship and the necessary funding for its first blockchain project.

But this exercise is not always enough: The permissioned network also might have to embark on a journey to uncover the correct incentive and economic model that will persuade enterprises to join a platform based on the notion of creation, distribution, and sharing of rewards benefiting all stakeholders.

Although not all conventional businesses and industries can blindly adopt the economic incentives of tokenomics, it is imperative that industries start the journey to explore the correct business model that will enable value creation and escalate the modernization efforts that many of today's industries desperately need to combat disruptive forces. The governance of blockchain networks includes various incentive economic models based on compliance costs and delegation of fiduciary response in a multiparty network. Development of a business model that ensures the longevity of the blockchain solution is as important as technology acumen and design consideration—and is an endeavor that requires careful analysis of the business of blockchain business models.

5

DEVELOPING A GOVERNANCE STRUCTURE FOR BLOCKCHAIN NETWORKS

A well-structured governance is the most crucial element of a successful business that drives excellence in performance and culture.

—Jai Singh Arun

Governance is concerned with rules of engagement for greater good and fairness in any system. Governance is also about rules and decision making in any system. Perhaps not surprisingly, if there are rules, there are also exceptions to those rules. Thus, governance is about coordinated decision making, and it manifests itself in different ways. For example, consensus enforces governance (equitable participation) by introducing economic incentives in trust systems, and in some cases the combination of a reputation system with consensus ensures integrity in participation.

No matter whether it is a self-governing or semi-autonomous structure, the governance of a blockchain business network defines a comprehensive set of rules, agreed to by participants, that ensure trust, transparency, control, and coordination by which the network is seamlessly designed, developed, tested, deployed, and operated. Figure 5.1 depicts the interactions that governance affects.

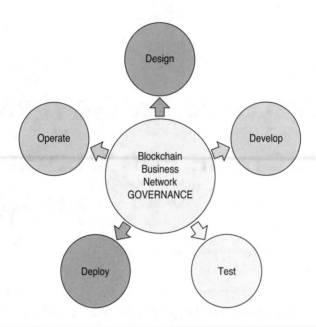

Figure 5.1 Governance across a blockchain-based business network.

In permissioned networks, governance becomes a design imperative that must be included as a part of the network's design. Also, it must be flexible and organic enough to morph with the ecosystem and membership changes and to respond to shifts in the business model. The technology constructs must support the dynamic nature of the governance structure and provide the least disruptive path to the collective decision-making process of the network participants. Because it permeates all aspects of the blockchain, governance is an integral component of a sustainable network.

The topic of governance imposes a collective set of challenges on both the process and political fronts. We can readily witness these challenges and the anatomy of governance structures in blockchain networks. The governance models range from self-governing networks to consortium-defined semi-autonomous governance structures. Finding the correct governance model to support the agenda of blockchain-based business networks is both an opportunity and a challenge. Indeed, governance presents an interesting paradox in the blockchain context.

As an example, consider a blockchain-presented value network that is self-governed and censorship-resistant, and whose governance structure is defined by control points and economic incentives to maintain a balance between network-based coordination and network-based decisions on transaction finality. The consensus algorithms of these decentralized networks present a distributed governance structure in which the input (transaction initiation) comes from various stakeholders (owners of assets, assigned or delegated ownership, simply delegated authority). This input consists of a transaction that goes through a series of network-based decentralized processing; the output is the decision, which takes the form of a transaction finality.

The governance structure is based on devised economic incentives that are driven by consensus and that govern the network. Thus, it is defined as the body (centralized or decentralized) whose sole responsibility is to make binding decisions in a system by establishing set of law or rules.

The genesis of blockchain relied upon technology-based systemic governance composed of incentives and mechanisms of coordination, as exemplified by the permissionless, crypto-asset–based networks operated by Bitcoin, Litecoin, and others. Nevertheless, this type of systemic governance poses a new set of challenges for enterprise business networks that attempt to use the tenets of blockchain technology. In the enterprise world, which is largely regulated and relies upon (mostly) permissioned blockchain models, the checks-and-balances system is complicated by transactions between competing entities, often with regulated data and a fiduciary responsibility, which cannot account for the tangible or systemically generated incentives (crypto assets) or have network-wide mechanisms of coordination due to privacy and confidentiality issues.

On the enterprise side of the divide, the focus should be on understanding the technology and reimagining the ecosystems, business network, regulatory compliance, confidentiality and privacy, and business models that impact industry networks. In this environment, the governance structure is an interesting challenge and emerging discipline. Indeed, in the enterprise blockchain world, the options range from full decentralization and quasi-decentralization to fully centralized blockchain networks—but the specific choice always hinges on the governance structure. The governance structure and landscape determine the interaction models, means of growth (centralized or decentralized), technology design, and overall business operations of the enterprise blockchain network. Figure 5.2 describes the differences between permissionless networks and permissioned enterprise-oriented networks.

Permissionless Networks		Permissioned Enterprise–Oriented Networks
Designing and implementing economic systems based in principles of decentralization, open or self-governance, and transparency		Technology-driven reimagining the ecosystems, business network, regulatory compliance, confidentiality and privacy, and business models
Creating crypto assets backed by real value		Implementing existing business process with blockchain
Building innovative technical solution	VS.	Creating proof of concept with quick results
Decentralized and disintermediation at the core		Involving existing intermediaries and central parties in developing common economic incentives
Economy-based incentives		Consortium-defined incentives and penalties
Network self-management and coordination		Consortium-defined semi-autonomous governance structures

Figure 5.2 Differences between permissionless and permissioned blockchain networks.

A blockchain-powered business network as digital transaction platform has the potential to facilitate the co-creation of new value and new synergies. It is a managed platform that is operated with a defined service level agreement (SLA), and has a robust governance structure that attracts new participants and sustains the confidence and business benefits of its founders and existing participants. It features a close-knit dependency on the business models and governance structure that oversee various facets of blockchain network operations. A well-thought-out governance structure for blockchain networks provides an important avenue for business continuity, funding and sourcing models, and overall growth, which is driven by the economic and financial structure of the business network and powered by the tenets of blockchain technology.

GOVERNANCE STRUCTURE AND LANDSCAPE

Systemic governance that relies solely on incentives and network coordination is inadequate to address more highly structured and regulated industries and their use cases. For this reason, we have taken the liberty of defining a governance structure and landscape that uses known and proven existing practices. The resulting model is modular and facilitates progression, yet also provides a layer that separates the competency concerns of the various participants.

The aim is to define a simplified governance framework that draws inspiration from the core tenets of blockchain design and incorporates a governance model that encompasses principles of game theory, incentives, penalties, flexibility, delegation, and network mechanisms of coordination. This framework uses blockchain technology to trust networks and flattens the distinction between the miner and the user. At the same time, it enforces rules of engagement that encourage technology upgrades and security updates and penalize noncompliant systems and nodes, including similar business network rules of engagement. The incentive mechanism is intended to ensure continued participation and resulting business benefits and growth for members of blockchain-powered business networks. This business governance model governs participation in business networks and an equitable cost structure that is fairly spread out among network members based on participant activity.

The three primary building blocks of a blockchain business network are technology infrastructure governance, network membership governance, and business network governance, as shown in Figure 5.3.

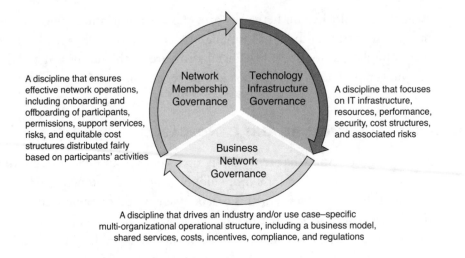

A discipline that ensures effective network operations, including onboarding and offboarding of participants, permissions, support services, risks, and equitable cost structures distributed fairly based on participants' activities

Network Membership Governance

Technology Infrastructure Governance

A discipline that focuses on IT infrastructure, resources, performance, security, cost structures, and associated risks

Business Network Governance

A discipline that drives an industry and/or use case–specific multi-organizational operational structure, including a business model, shared services, costs, incentives, compliance, and regulations

Figure 5.3 Governance disciplines for a blockchain-based business network.

TECHNOLOGY INFRASTRUCTURE GOVERNANCE

Technology infrastructure governance is a discipline that focuses on IT infrastructures, performance, cost structures, technology, and business risks. It includes a set of collaborative tools, processes, and methodologies intended to ensure organizational alignment of the business strategy with the technology infrastructure and services.

The goal of technology infrastructure governance is to support, adapt, and complement the blockchain business network's objectives. In a blockchain network, as opposed to a centralized entity, these tasks can be challenging because the governance framework should focus on specifying an accountability framework to encourage necessary behavior. In this setting, the functioning of the IT infrastructure that enables deployment and operation of that infrastructure is defined as the foundational layer of the blockchain network. Many best practices frameworks, such as Information Technology Infrastructure Library (ITIL) and Governance, Risk, and Compliance (GRC), have already laid a strong foundation for blockchain networks to build upon and create a blockchain-specific technology governance structure.

Any technical design should accommodate the flexibility of various participants when it comes to choices related to technology and infrastructure. Blockchain networks will generally aim for certain levels of decentralization or quasi-decentralization. In turn, IT governance should accommodate a model that supports distributed flexibility and distributed control.

Technology governance–related tasks include the following:

1. Devise a decentralized IT management structure.
2. Devise a model for distributed (and decentralized) maintenance, including software and hardware updates, upgrades, and path management.
3. Devise a framework that uses industry standards, such as COBIT, ITIL, ISO, CMMI, and FAIR, that are driven by the consortium, joint venture, or other business model.
4. Establish industry-specific governance, risk, and compliance (GRC) tools.
5. Perform consortium resource optimization, which includes choices related to technology procurement, supplier–vendor relations, SLA management, skills, and talent management.
6. Perform technology adoption and risk assessment, which requires keeping up with technology evolution and economic deployment models, including deployment and operational risks.
7. Devise a network deployment strategy. This task is not as simple as an application upgrade. Include a model that can encourage and enforce continual technology and security updates and upgrades.
8. Set up network support services, which are business networks. The governance model should include network support services, IT SLA enforcement, and membership services.
9. Perform consortium risk optimization, which includes operational support services (OSSs) and business support services (BSSs), IT infrastructure continuity services and planning, and technology alignment to legal and regulatory requirements, among other factors.

The IT governance model should encourage technology upgrades and security, and penalize noncompliant systems and nodes, so as to create an incentive mechanism to ensure continuous participation. Figure 5.4 provides a quick checklist of key elements that should be considered in technology infrastructure governance.

Technology Infrastructure Governance Checklist
Distributed IT management structure
Model of distributed maintenance
Framework for utilizing industry standards
Resource optimization
Technology assessment and adoption
Network deployment
Network support services
Risk optimization

Figure 5.4 Technology governance elements.

NETWORK MEMBERSHIP GOVERNANCE

The model of network governance in a blockchain network reflects the fact that the network is organic and composed of ecosystem players with varied business interests. In essence, it is an interactive ecosystem with common business objectives instead of a bureaucratic structure with a centralized business entity.

This model imposes extraordinary challenges on network members to maintain the balance of smooth business operation and the enforcement of engagement rules within the operating framework. In many consortium-led business structures, network governance might involve a select set of autonomous entities that are engaged in creating value, services, and digital goods, and it might use smart contracts and the blockchain as a marketplace mechanism to coordinate and safeguard the exchange of value. Therefore, the business model plays a critical role in increasing the efficiency of the operating model and reducing agency problems due to defined rules of engagement associated with both rewards and penalties.

These business governance models govern participation in business networks and create an equitable cost structure that is fairly distributed among members based on participant activity. Their structure enables autonomous and like-minded business entities to engage in business transactions, contracts, and value creation. To ensure smooth operation of the blockchain, the governance structure should include rules of engagement and social contracts that promote fair behavior and reputation systems to enforce it.

Blockchain network membership governance–related activities include the following:

1. **Membership onboarding and offboarding:** The permissioning structure and key management can include a model that has the following qualities:
   a. Vote-driven but centrally managed
   b. Has a federated structure in which members invite other business entities to join the network
   c. Has a delegated structure that includes services providers that can delegate to other members
2. An equitable and fair cost structure.
3. Consortium-wide data ownership structure for business entities joining and leaving the network.
4. Compliance assurance services for industry-specific regulatory oversight provisioning, which includes a model to act as a delegate to generate regulatory compliance, adherence, and reporting.
5. A dispute resolution charter for the network.
6. Coordination and direction of the technology infrastructure and management.

7. Business network and SLA management for the blockchain business network management.

8. **Network support services:** Business networks. The governance model should include network support services, business network SLA enforcement, and membership services.

9. **Network-specific risk optimization:** A business support services structure that includes business continuity services and planning, network alignment to legal and regulatory requirements, and other items.

Figure 5.5 provides a quick checklist of key elements that should be considered in network membership governance.

Network Membership Governance Checklist
Member onboarding/offboarding
Equitable and fair cost structure
Data ownership structure
Regulatory oversight provisioning
Permission structure
Service level agreement (SLA) management
Network support services
Risk optimization
Network operations

Figure 5.5 Network membership governance elements.

BUSINESS NETWORK GOVERNANCE

Business networks that are powered by blockchain need a governance model that is industry- and use case–specific. Also, these networks must account for various facets of the industry itself, as well as its evolution— including the change in overall governance structure. Blockchain is an important form of multi-organizational governance. Its core objective is to increase operational efficiency and reduce hurdles imposed by the agency (centralized business entity). The efficiency is enhanced by distributed data, asset- and value-related decision making, and decentralized problem solving through trust systems and consensus.

The term *shared governance* is often used to describe a business activity that collectively represents an industry to the various external ecosystems, such as adjunct business networks, and governmental and regulatory entities. This collective representation has advantages such as sharing of the business process costs and the market benefits conferred by arbitrage, brokerage, and attracting new ecosystem players.

One key goal of business network governance is to manage the growth of the network while maintaining the SLA and core business objectives. The governance structure includes a wider understanding of network functions, with these collective functions by various participants then leading to network outcomes. As blockchain networks evolve and grow and as new participants are added or removed, the dynamics of the network change, and both bilateral and multilateral relationships may emerge.

Co-creation is a concept that brings different parties together (e.g., a company and a group of customers) to jointly produce a mutually valued outcome. Co-creation gathers a unique blend of ideas from direct customers or viewers (who are not the direct users of the product), which then leads to a plethora of new ideas for the organizations that represent the consortium. Ideally, business network governance imperatives will seek to balance the growth and cultivate the synergies between the ecosystems so as to transform the business network by adopting new business models.

Business network governance–related tenets include the following items:

- **Communication and notification:** Network-related charter and communication.
- **Synthesis of transaction costs and economies of scale:** Common and shared services management, such as know your customer (KYC), audits, reporting, network operations, IT infrastructure, and flattened business processes.

- **Business SLAs:** Quality assurance, performance, and network security.
- **Favorable exchange conditions:** Integrity of digital assets, asset specificity, supply and demand uncertainty, and product and business network evolution.
- **Collective representation:** Enforcement of industry-specific compliance legal and regulatory frameworks.
- **Structural embeddedness:** Adherence to industry-specific requirements for trusted movement of assets and value in the network.
- **Federated governance framework:** Framework, charter, and stewards of technology and network membership governance frameworks.
- **Business structure:** Formulation of appropriate business models, legal charters, and rules of engagement for network business operations.

Figure 5.6 provides a quick checklist of key elements that should be considered in business network governance.

Business Network Governance Checklist

- Network charter and management
- Common/shared services management
- Business service level agreement: quality assurance, performance, and network security management
- Business exchange conditions management
- Industry-specific requirements, legal and regulatory compliance adherence
- Business operations structure

Figure 5.6 Business network governance elements.

Development of governance structure is a challenging and emerging discipline in the enterprise blockchain world, where the debate around the spectrum of options—which range from full decentralization and quasi-decentralization to fully centralized blockchain networks—hinges on the governance structure selected. The governance structure and landscape determine the interaction models, growth (centralized or decentralized), technology design, and overall business operation of enterprise blockchain networks. The platform that facilitates co-creation and new synergies must be effectively managed, operate under the aegis of defined SLAs, and have a robust governance structure that attracts new participants and sustains the confidence and business benefits of its founders and existing participants.

There is a close-knit dependency between business models and governance structures that govern various facets of blockchain network operations. A well-crafted governance model will ensure balance and smooth interactions between various entities that compete with some network participants and that cooperate and co-create with some other network participants.

Although blockchain networks are decentralized by nature, the governance structure is fundamentally driven by the type of the business model (including business participants, outcomes, and incentives) that you are considering for your blockchain business network. As discussed in Chapter 4, these potential models include a joint venture, consortium, NewCo, business ecosystem, founder-led network (build, own, and operate), or founding consortium–led network (build, own, operate, and transfer).

In addition, governance models can be self-governed or semi-autonomous, managed off-chain or on-chain. *Off-chain* means that governance rules and policies are managed outside the blockchain; that is, after they are reviewed and approved, they are implemented on blockchain. *On-chain* means that governance policies and rules are managed by using smart contracts and consensus algorithms within the blockchain.

In the next section, we review an example of a governance structure in a blockchain. This structure is based on a global digital supply chain network that we refer to as *SCTrustNet*.

SCTRUSTNET

The SCTrustNet network is intended to bring end-to-end visibility, trust, transparency, and transformation to a consortium-led business model of an enterprise supply chain network, which consists of various participants including suppliers, buyers, banks, shipping carriers, freight forwarders, and regulators (custom and port authorities). As shown in Figure 5.7, the transformational business outcomes are expected to reduce cost, complexity, and latency across supply chain transactions and network.

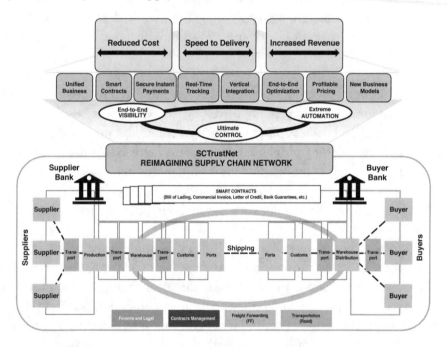

Figure 5.7 SCTrustNet governance structure.

The SCTrustNet governance structure is organized into three primary areas: business network, network membership, and technology infrastructure. Let us dive into the details of each of these areas.

BUSINESS NETWORK GOVERNANCE

The supply chain business-specific legal and financial policies and rules are governed and managed by the business network governance structure. They include the following items:

- A unified charter includes the overall network's business outcomes, participants' contributions (costs, resources, and ecosystem), and their incentives (visibility, control, efficiency, and monetary rewards) in SCTrustNet.

- The agreed business model is a consortium-led ecosystem with a set of founding members (three suppliers, three buyers, two banks, and a shipping line carrier) and nonfounding members (freight forwarders and custom and port authorities).

- Founding members can order and endorse the transaction for validation and commitment. Nonfounding members can only endorse transactions.

- Business contracts (purchase orders, bills of lading, letters of credit, bank guarantees, commercial invoices, and others) between buyers, suppliers, banks, and carriers are managed by using smart contracts.

- SLAs for shared services, such as reporting, auditing, tracking, and tracing of assets, including penalties in quality of service, are coded on-chain.

- Cross-border trader and payments regulations and compliance policies are agreed to between buyers and suppliers and added to smart contracts for transaction and fulfillment agility.

- Business operations and security principles to ensure participants' and their data's privacy, integrity, and performance are part of the digital supply chain network.

- Risk identification and mitigation policies are included in SCTrustNet.

NETWORK MEMBERSHIP GOVERNANCE

Network membership governance drives the overall membership management and governance of the network participants, network services, and related activities. It includes the following items:

- Established rules for each type of participant, the authority to invite entities to join the network, and onboarding and offboarding of new suppliers, buyers, freight forwarders, banks, carriers, and custom and port authorities
- Access and operations rights to data and transactions (purchase orders, invoices, bills of lading, and letters of credit) in the blockchain
- Membership and network participation fee structures for each type of participant and their roles
- Management of decentralized and shared network services, including track and trace, purchase order processing, and transportation
- Penalties for not delivering services and quality and neglecting the charter of SCTrustNet
- Communication policies to share the correct information with the correct participants at the correct time in the supply chain for trust and transparency

NETWORK INFRASTRUCTURE GOVERNANCE

The infrastructure governance for SCTrustNet includes all the rules and regulations of the following items:

- Blockchain technology (i.e., Corda, Ethereum, and Hyperledger Fabric) assessment, selection, and deployment (public and private cloud)
- Setting up blockchain nodes (a system with a copy of the distributed ledger and connected in the network)
- Project management, test, and deployment of chaincodes (decentralized applications) for network services
- Security and access of nodes and shared services chaincodes

- Autonomous execution of incentives and penalties for infrastructure service and quality assurance, and risk management
- SCTrustNet infrastructure operations (server, storage, and network)
- Change, upgrade, and release management of the technology
- High availability, disaster recovery, and business continuity management
- Capacity, scalability, and performance management policies
- Incidence management, logging, and monitoring

CHAPTER SUMMARY

Blockchain-based application networks are more than a technical project implementation. In our case deployment observations, the technical aspects of the blockchain, if they are well designed by using the correct skills, can be realized with a high certainty of success. To achieve this success, we need to carry out a series of business-driven activities that ensure the correct focus, enterprise resources, acumen, and organizational energy are channeled with executive commitment.

Selecting the correct use case is necessary to understand the appropriate business models and define the correct governance structure. This choice puts the focus on enterprise commitment and industry-wide influence as a means to attract other ecosystem players, which then commit to the common vision and goals of the blockchain network. The use case and resulting business economics drive the investment agenda, which enables the enterprise or consortium to focus on business models that lead to equitable and sustainable deployment and a governance structure that meets the industry-specific requirements.

Blockchain projects encompass creative strategic thinking and solve complex technology problems, which means that the correct use case must have a tight linkage between the business models and the technology blueprint. The governance model integrates a business model with the correct amount of coordination, thereby ensuring that all participants adhere to a common set of objectives, fair and equitable use of network resources, and rules of engagement.

ENTERPRISE STRUCTURES IN A DECENTRALIZED ECONOMY

Many modern organizations in the current economic structure strive to achieve monopolistic profit gains. In doing so, they may create competition that inadvertently nurtures intermediaries that drive higher costs and lower the quality of goods and services that are offered to the consumers. Conversely, a decentralized economy challenges the status quo with a new paradigm of peer-to-peer exchange and shared gains. This new shift might not be applicable to all enterprises that are adopting blockchain technology in their business use cases and industry processes, so you must choose a right organizational structure from among the choices of centralized, decentralized, and hybrid economies.

CENTRALIZED STRUCTURE

In a centralized structure, enterprises work toward concentrating the power and authority of the business network and the legal policies, procedures, and operations. The communication and decision-making power traverse in a top-down direction. This approach is a good choice for making faster decisions and executing business transaction validation and commits in the ledgers, but it might not enhance collaboration, innovation, and efficiency in the network.

The primary roles in enterprises within a centralized structure are hierarchical, and responsibilities are divided in a way that produces an inflexible environment for co-development and limits motivation. The business execution logic in these enterprises is tightly coupled and controlled to ensure the stability of the system, which leaves the system vulnerable to a single point of failure.

Among the most popular centralized structure-based enterprises today are Google and Facebook. In these organizations' operations, all Internet transactions are directed toward a centralized system or platform.

DECENTRALIZED STRUCTURE

In a decentralized structure, authority and control are distributed across the enterprises that participate in the blockchain business network (Figure 6.1). The business functions are loosely coupled so that execution can be faster, but making a unified decision or achieving consensus might become a time-consuming activity. Creating an environment conducive to co-developing and sharing the gains is the primary intent of decentralized structures.

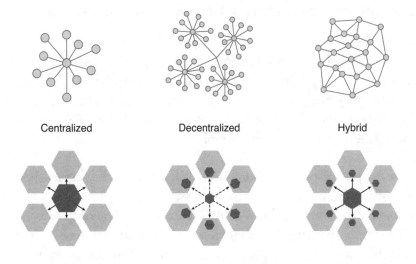

Centralized   Decentralized   Hybrid

Figure 6.1 Enterprise structures in a decentralized economy.

Unlike a centralized system, a decentralized system does not require all the transactions to pass through a single platform. Instead, many nodes in the system can perform peer-to-peer actions. BitTorrent is a typical example of a decentralized structure where a peer-to-peer file sharing protocol is used to distribute data and electronic files over the Internet.

HYBRID STRUCTURE

The hybrid structure is the most suitable environment for many enterprises that want to leverage the value of blockchain from an autonomy perspective, but also need to maintain authority and control over certain aspects of the platform and network. With such a structure, no central entity reviews and validates business transactions within the network. Instead, the blockchain network consists of enterprises that have either a centralized or decentralized structure. Many of the blockchain consortia today employ a hybrid structure in which the decentralization of transactional information provides speed, transparency, and auditability, but can also provide high throughput.

ROLES OF AN ENTERPRISE IN A BLOCKCHAIN NETWORK

Major industries are regulated in terms of business transactions and data privacy compliance requirements. The enterprises within these industries cannot adopt a public blockchain network. Instead, private or permissioned blockchain networks are the preferred choices for enterprises that can balance their business needs with their needs for technology innovation, and for regulation and compliance.

When a private or permissioned blockchain network is established to transform an industry business process, enterprises may play various roles depending on their business goals and network value outcomes (Figure 6.2). For example, these roles might include those of a founder, member, operator, or general user of a network or consortium. In addition, some of the roles can be combined or further disjoined in a network based on the stage, maturity, scale, industry, business process, and use case.

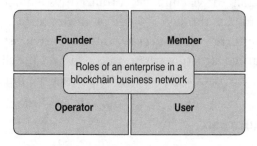

Figure 6.2 Roles of an enterprise in a blockchain network.

FOUNDERS

Founder enterprises have identified a business transformation or disruptive use case or process. They have a clear vision for the blockchain network, its participants, business benefits, and costs, and how it can be designed, built, operated, managed, and governed. Founders assume the responsibility of inviting the appropriate participating enterprises and sharing the vision and business value of the network to encourage participation.

Pragmatically, it is best if a consortium has only one or very few founders, so as to assure better control and management. However, this setup defeats the purpose of decentralization in the network—that is, the autonomy of the other participants.

Hundreds of blockchain consortia have been built over the past few years. R3 is an example of a founder of a consortium that includes more than 200 financial institutes, regulators, banks, and other enterprises.

MEMBERS

Member enterprises are members of a blockchain network along with the founding enterprises. They might have joined the network either as a founding member or after the network is established. Member enterprises have a blockchain node that is called a *peer*, which means they have a copy of the ledger and can run chaincode and participate in the consensus process if they are authorized by founders or other governing enterprises, based on consortium policies and rules. Members share the costs and benefits of network design, construction, and deployment. As the network grows and the members' contributions, roles, and responsibilities change, they can become founding enterprises.

Financial institutes such as JPMC, Credit Suisse, RBS, and UBS are members of the R3 consortium.

OPERATORS

The operator of a blockchain network can be a founder or member enterprise. Alternatively, it can be a third-party enterprise that assumes responsibility for the network operations and technology management for a fee that is based on the transactions volume or a fixed monthly or annual fee. If the operator is not a member or founder, then it might not be given access and visibility to the business transactions in the network. It might have a copy of a distributed ledger, but only for performing operating tasks. The operator enterprise maintains service level agreements (SLAs) regarding the operations quality, and the performance and availability of the network.

USERS

The users of a blockchain network are invited and enabled by the founders and members. Depending on the users' permission level, they can access or view part of the transactions and network information, but they do not own data. For example, regulators and auditors may become users of a network so that they can view network transactions and ensure that compliance guidelines are met.

Users might pay a fee for network access and participation based on an agreed plan with the network founder and members. As general users continue to contribute and bring value to network, they may become members per the governance policies and guidelines.

BUILDING AN EFFECTIVE TEAM

To build an effective team for a blockchain project and business network, you must ensure that the following items are identified and defined (Figure 6.3):

- **Project enterprise:** Is your organization a start-up enterprise that is building a new business solution or network by using blockchain, or is it part of an existing enterprise that has identified an industry process or business use case for blockchain?

- **Type of a network:** Will the blockchain network be led by the founder enterprise(s) or by consortium members?
- **Roles of participating enterprises in the network:** Are the enterprises founders, members, operators, or users?
- **Technology:** Will the network use enterprise-ready blockchain technologies like Hyperledger or Ethereum, or will the founder build its own?
- **Network infrastructure:** Will the network use cloud environments that are provided by major vendors, or will your enterprise build its own private cloud or on-premises infrastructure?
- **Scope:** Do you have MVP and MVE requirements and limits?

The answers to these questions can help you identify the requirements for the key network activities, roles, responsibilities, and corresponding team members and skills.

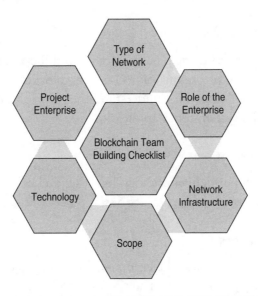

Figure 6.3 Blockchain team building checklist.

PROJECT TEAM ROLES

A typical blockchain project team requires all or some of the key roles described in this section. Some of these roles may be combined depending on the project enterprise, type of network, roles of participating enterprises, technology, and network infrastructure.

Steering Committee Members

Steering committee members are individuals from enterprises that are part of the network. They direct the management and governance of the overall blockchain network, business and legal policies, rules, and regulations.

Legal Consultants

Legal counsel is crucial in the blockchain project and network. Legal consultants provide advice about how legal partnerships and contracts are defined for the automated execution of smart contracts and how to structure initial coin offerings (ICOs) from a compliance regulation perspective.

Blockchain Consultants

Blockchain consultants help businesses adopt blockchain technology and build the network of organizations by using blockchain applications and solutions. Consultants must understand the principles of blockchain technology, the systems, and applications.

Crypto Developer

A crypto developer defines and develops the level of security and encryption strength required for transactions and network security.

Project Managers

Project managers manage the entire blockchain project life cycle, including schedules, costs, and budget. They control and oversee work items and process activities, and define tasks and deliverables for other roles.

Product Owners

Product owners manage the overall vision—that is, the roadmap for the development and delivery of the product, features, and functions based on the business requirements of the blockchain network. They also are responsible for the profit and loss of the product.

User Researchers

User researchers identify a problem or pain point for a user in the context of an industry or business use case transformation. In addition, they develop the user requirements and user behaviors related to the blockchain network.

User Experience Designers

User experience (UX) designers write user stories. They enable a seamless experience for users by specifying simplified interfaces and information that is presented from the blockchain system and network.

Blockchain Architect

The blockchain architect defines the system architecture, including how the nodes (computers) are deployed in a blockchain network and how everyone agrees by consensus whether the transactions are valid.

System Architect

The system architect defines how the system operates in a blockchain network by incorporating input from the blockchain architect, designer, product owner, and developers.

Blockchain Developers

Blockchain developers program the logic of business networks into chaincode and application user interfaces. These developers should be proficient in JavaScript or have golang (Go programming language) programming skills.

Quality or Test Engineer

Quality or test engineers evaluate each function, feature, application, and overall blockchain system by using various input parameters and conditions to identify any defects. The goal is for the developer to fix these defects before the product is put into a production environment.

Network Engineer

Network engineers ensure that peer-to-peer networking works at scale in a blockchain. They make sure that data and information are communicated or exchanged efficiently to the intended recipient only.

Business Development Manager

The business development manager's task is to forge business partnerships across the ecosystem, with or without participation of those enterprises in a blockchain network. The manager also develops sales proposals and presents them to potential customers and partner organizations to encourage them to participate in the network.

Marketing Manager or Leader

Marketing managers or leaders develop and create a go-to market and thought leadership strategy, which consists of crisp and clear messaging for various market segments and geographies. They also create marketing collateral and reference materials and brief industry analyses for brand leadership.

INTRAPRISE SYNERGY

As you build a blockchain project team, you might realize that all the roles are not part of a single enterprise in a business network. Instead, those roles are located within the enterprises that have most expertise and knowledge and bring differentiated added-value. However, all the teams and team members are logically and geographically different from those enterprises that are collaborating and co-developing to achieve a common business goal.

This concept of bringing the "best of the best" from each enterprise together within an ecosystem is called *intraprise synergy*. Intraprise synergy creates a fundamental shift in business by empowering the blockchain business network participants with decentralized authority and autonomy to design, develop, test, and deliver the best of their skills as part of a broader system and network. It inherently motivates many enterprises to deliver continuously and realize shared gains.

Intraprise synergy that is developed in a decentralized environment disrupts many traditional business processes and systems by optimizing the efficiency of co-creation and co-development, which eliminates various unnecessary intermediaries. Imagine this environment as a large and autonomous network with decentralized power spread among multiple geographies and network operation centers. As depicted in Figure 6.4, the intraprise synergy concept drives federation across a decentralized environment.

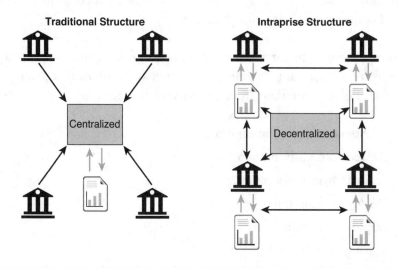

Figure 6.4 Intraprise synergy.

AN EXAMPLE OF A BLOCKCHAIN PROJECT TEAM

As mentioned earlier, the requirements for the blockchain project team depend on the business model, the ecosystem, and—most importantly—the role of your enterprise in the business network. These elements help determine which roles, responsibilities, and skills are required as part of building the right team for the blockchain project.

In this section, we'll use a blockchain-based supply chain network project team as our example. The network is focused on building a trusted, transparent, and secure digital supply chain. Beside the steering committee, business development, marketing management, and legal and business consultants, the technical team described in the following subsections is needed to build the solution.

BLOCKCHAIN TECHNOLOGY SOLUTION TEAM

The technical team for a blockchain project identifies technical requirements from a business network, selects a suitable blockchain technology, and develops requirement-specific application chaincode, smart contracts, and consensus policies into programs.

As an example, to carry out the development, test, and operations functions for a large supply chain business network solution, a technical team consisting of more than 28 members was needed:

- **Architecture team:** minimum 2
- **Design team:** minimum 5
- **Security team:** minimum 2
- **DevOps:** minimum 3
- **Deployment:** minimum 4
- **Testing:** minimum 7
- **Specialists:** at least 1 for each technology
- **Project manager or project management office (PMO) function:** minimum 3

CHAPTER SUMMARY

This chapter has described the essential elements for building a team to drive a blockchain project. Various types of enterprise structures may be employed in a decentralized economy—centralized, decentralized, and hybrid. Potential roles for an enterprise within a blockchain network include being a founder, member, operator, and user.

To build an effective team for a blockchain project and business network, you must ensure that the project network, type of network, roles of the participating enterprises in the network, technology, network infrastructure, and scope are identified and defined. A typical blockchain project team requires all or some of the following key roles: steering committee members, legal consultants, blockchain consultants, crypto developer, project managers, product owners, user researchers, user experience designers, blockchain architect, system architect, blockchain developers, quality or test engineer, network engineer, business development manager, and marketing manager or leader.

The goal of bringing the "best of the best" from each enterprise in an ecosystem is to yield intraprise synergy. This synergy empowers the blockchain business network participants with decentralized authority and autonomy to design, develop, test, and deliver the best of their skills as part of broader system and network. Moreover, it inherently motivates many enterprises to deliver continuously and realize shared gains.

7

Understanding Financial Models, Investment Rubrics, and Model Risk Frameworks

In blockchain, decentralization manifests in the corporate structure, technology governance, GRC policy frameworks, and all the constructs of the financial model, from investment rubric to ROI modeling.

—Nitin Gaur

Although technology design and business models dominate planning and conversation related to blockchain projects, understanding the blockchain monetization strategy is an important and fruitful exercise for any business contemplating a blockchain project. The monetization strategy is a difficult problem to solve for both permissioned and permissionless blockchain networks due to the lack of maturity (and thus standardization) of technology design and emerging business models that aim to use the technology landscape. Blockchain technology has introduced new design configurations, data authentication, security, and data distribution and trust mechanisms that might evolve as a narrative during the Internet's next era. This narrative invites comparison to the original Internet era, in which new businesses and the resulting economies were created; the upcoming era, however, will focus on value creation and transfer instead of just information exchange.

Although the notion of a flattened shared business process, distributed record keeping, and smart contracts replacing business rules might seem an unrealistic model for an established enterprise, it can create a tremendous opportunity. In particular, it enables the enterprise to divide transactions to the nth decimal point, which makes microtransactions feasible. This feasibility supports the ecosystem is rethinking monetization, through possibilities ranging from peer-to-peer to machine-to-machine transactions.

While blockchain itself provides the technology constructs to facilitate exchange, ownership, and trust in the network, it is in the digitization of value elements that asset tokenization becomes truly essential. Tokenization is the process of converting the assets and rights or claims to an asset into a digital representation, or token, within a blockchain network. This distinction between cryptocurrency and tokenized assets is important to understanding the exchange vehicles, valuation models, and fungibility across the various value networks that are emerging in the blockchain world. In particular, tokenization poses interoperability challenges regarding the technical and business issues surrounding equitable swaps.

Tokenization of assets can lead to the creation of a business model that fuels fractional ownership or the ability to own an instance of a large asset. The promised asset tokenization on blockchain-based business networks includes digitization, solving the inefficiencies of time and trust, and creating new business models and facilitating co-creation through the synergies of the network participants.

The monetizing dilemma is one of perspective. The disruptors are focused on microtransactions (a claim on an instance as opposed to the whole asset), initial coin offerings (ICOs), and security token offerings (STOs), which address fundraising needs. In contrast, the enterprise is focused on efficiency, cost savings, shared costs of business processes, and other factors. This diversity adds an interesting tangent to the quest to create an ecosystem that can be both robust and symbiotic.

The following monetization strategies are often employed by the ecosystem:

- **Token-based models:** Operation fees are used to write to the blockchain-powered business network's distributed database.
- **Tokens as a medium of exchange:** Tokens are traded, lent, or sold as a step-through currency.
- **Asset-pair trading:** Margins are monetized.
- **Commercialization of the protocol:** Technology services are monetized, including cloud and software, lab, and consulting services.

An individual monetization strategy must be selected to drive the investment rubric of blockchain projects and all related financial modeling, including financial considerations, the return on investment (ROI) model, the risk model, the risk framework, and the overall investment rubric. The chosen strategy, in turn, serves as a guide to define the progress, risk, and expected outcome of the project.

UNDERSTANDING BLOCKCHAIN PROJECT FINANCIAL FUNDAMENTALS

Blockchain-based networks offer the opportunity to develop new business and trust models, which is why the phrase "revolutionary potential" is appropriate when referring to blockchain. These networks' ability to support multiparty collaboration related to shared, trusted data and process automation across organizational boundaries brings benefits to many levels, starting with efficiency gains and culminating in reinvention of how entire industry ecosystems operate.

Blockchain initiatives fall into two main categories:

- **Improvements of existing process flows.** Good use case candidates include the following:
  - Any scenario that involves multiple parties that are wasting time and resources reconciling data when they should be viewing the same data

- Situations where fraud may arise due to a lack of timely information
- Processes where efficiency gains and other benefits can be achieved if all participants have visibility across an entire supply or value chain
- **New business and service models.** Most of these models have not been invented yet, but we can see emerging enterprise blockchain networks that open new markets (such as affordable trade finance for smaller businesses) or rethink how individuals, public authorities, and business interact without compromising data privacy and commercial confidentiality, and minimizing fraud risk.[1]

Figure 7.1 describes how as size of blockchain network grows, the business impact grows correspondingly in the industry and economy.

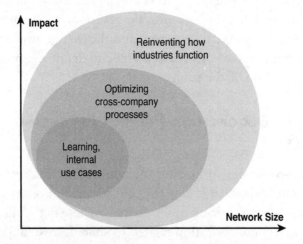

Figure 7.1 Blockchain network sizes and corresponding impacts.

The idea of applying a structured and systematic approach to assessing blockchain financial fundamentals might seem like an obvious task. Due to the complex technology landscape, the decentralized nature of network operations, and the resulting business model, however, additional considerations may arise regarding the use of proven techniques and tools that force us to rethink the financial fundamentals.

One approach to deal with the nascent blockchain technology and the evolving blockchain landscape is to assess the key characteristics of the key projects and identify the weakest link in the transaction network. We can employ proven qualitative and quantitative tools and measures to identify and discern the key risks. These risks can then be interpreted, and their impact and severity determined and prioritized, which will lead to a well-organized analysis of project financial factors.

Building a financial model usually starts with the process of building a business design around a new business stream or transforming an existing business stream with the goal of reducing costs through more efficient operations. After the business design is defined, the task of designing a financial model then includes indicators such as the following:

- **The ROI model of the project:** The valuation models that are inputs into the investment decision-making process.
- **Partnership funding models:** The sources of funds that are based on participants, founding partners, and consortium models.
- **Business structure:** An equitable economic model of the network that incentivizes investment and participation, and equally benefits the eco-system players.
- **The rate of return to the founding partners, consortium, and network operators:** The model that provides an equitable structure on ROI.
- **Financing:** Debt, equity, and other models that might be necessary for the initial investment and operations while imposing a financial risk to the network infrastructure.
- **Governance, risk, and compliance (GRC) and model risk framework:** Focus on financial liability and risk due to regulatory, compliance, and other risk elements.

Blockchain financial models are unlike many project financial models because blockchain-powered business networks contain an ecosystem, marketplaces, and a network of business-centric participants that often belong to the same industry and both compete and collaborate with each other. This model creates complexity in the business structure of the network. In particular, a single entity-driven network cannot be viewed as competitive by participants. Moreover, such a model induces centralized control, which is regarded as the antithesis to the decentralized control structure that blockchain promotes as a fundamental tenet. In blockchain, decentralization manifests in the corporate structure, technology governance, GRC policy frameworks, and all the constructs of the financial model, from investment rubric to ROI modeling. To achieve the desired ends, you must establish a specific business structure (consortium, joint venture, or other) and then devise frameworks for risk, governance, and operations before working on the financial model.

This approach addresses the political and relationship structure, and the investment and risk appetite, of the founders. To be successful, however, a consortium (a group of entities that cooperate and share resources to achieve a common objective) must have a clear and equitable financial and operating model. The funding sources, partnership structure, initial cost of investment, risk, business valuation, total addressable market of the network, regulatory burden, compliance, and related costs are inputs into the financial model analysis, as depicted in Figure 7.2.

Thus, building a financial model usually starts with creating a business design around a new business stream or transforming an existing one with the goal of achieving cost reductions by adopting efficient operations. Blockchain injects complexity into this picture, owing to the decentralized control structure that blockchain promotes as a fundamental tenet. This decentralization affects the corporate structure, technology governance, GRC policy frameworks, and other constructs of the financial model, such as investment rubrics and ROI modeling. You must establish a specific business structure (consortium, joint venture, or other) and devise frameworks for risk, governance, and operations before working on the financial model.

Figure 7.2 Key elements of a financial model analysis for a blockchain network.

BLOCKCHAIN INVESTMENT RUBRIC

It is vital for an enterprise to establish an investment rubric as a risk mitigation technique. An investment rubric is a layered abstraction that represents the investment criteria and landscape. The rubric evaluation criteria have inputs, outputs, and continual analysis. The inputs are generally assumptions that drive the model, such as technology design, architecture and talent acquisition, compliance costs, and cost-efficient versus new business opportunity models. The outputs are the projected performance metrics that are measured against the stated input objectives.

The investment rubric also can serve as a model that you can use to evaluate multiple sets of performance metrics with different assumptions.

This investment rubric is both a guide and an evaluation tool for blockchain projects. The continual assets of the rubric define the merits of a potential investment and objectify the decision and justification of that investment. The rubric is a financial model that employs various business valuation techniques, such as net present value (NPV), benefit–cost ratio (BCR), internal rate of return (IRR), and GRC. Governance risk management and compliance analysis, which provide a holistic investment and risk profile, are not considered at the proof-of-concept phase.

Devising a comprehensive investment profile and model is a significant step in communicating to investors, business partners, and stakeholders the extent and depth of an analysis with a clear defensible plan for project execution, deployment, and subsequent risk mitigation that is embedded at every layer of the rubric. You can use the investment rubric as an important tool for modeling and analysis with a feedback loop mechanism. The tool is used as a scoring guide to evaluate the intended investment objective and stated outcome.

The idea behind this approach is to have a progressive development model that includes risk mitigation through continual tweaking of models to achieve the needed objectives. This model starts from proof points at the early stages of technology experimentation, and progresses to more serious efforts concerning business models and establishing a minimum viable ecosystem (MVE) while testing the risk, ROI, and financial and governance model. With new knowledge and incremental success at every stage, applying and tweaking the valuation models and risk models and establishing autonomic (sense and response) governance policies lead to growth and the scaling of the blockchain-powered business ecosystem. In summary, the investment rubric is a sophisticated tool to measure performance objectives, as depicted in Figure 7.3.

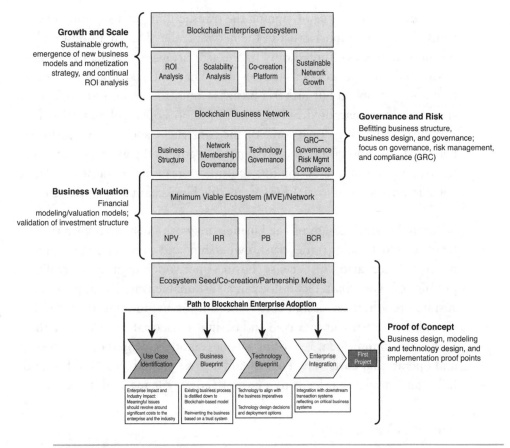

Figure 7.3 Investment rubric.

The elements of the blockchain investment rubric are discussed next.

PROOF OF CONCEPT OR DESIGN

A proof of concept (PoC) or design is a tool to mitigate project risk by testing the feasibility of the blockchain network design. In blockchain enterprise adoption, we must ensure that we have a microscopic focus on a singular use case and distill the existing business into a blockchain paradigm.

As we debate the merits of signing the transactions versus mining the transactions to establish trust in the network, the blockchain-powered business network is limited only by the aspirations of the member businesses and their networks as they evolve. That is, the key factor is not a technology problem but rather a business ambition issue. A deep focus on sustainability is paradoxical because it promotes open collaborative innovation while locking down some of the constructs, such as consensus or trust systems, and governance systems that govern the assets, smart contracts, and overall interaction in a multiparty transaction network. These considerations are essential for sustainable blockchain system design.

Successful system design of the business network must align with the tenets of blockchain (trade, trust, ownership, and transactionality in a multiparty scenario). Otherwise, business networks might never realize the promise of blockchain technology in a sustainable way. To support and sustain growth, these design considerations are paramount. Initial and thoughtful investment in a PoC and design is essential to sustaining the long-term commitment regarding business models, capital commitment, and operational costs. The PoC should also be viewed as a "fail fast and fail often" model that leads to a cost-effective agile methodology.

BUSINESS VALUATION

Blockchain is all about creating shared value. During the initial design phase, it is essential for founders to invite their identified MVE members to participate in discussions regarding the incentives structure, the way in which the network will operate, and the expected roles and responsibilities of each member.

Business valuation is an important task and a natural transition from technology and design proof points. The challenge of business valuation lies in identifying the appropriate valuation methodology and tools, determining funding and partnership models, devising equitable participation models (founders, normal participants, and added-value participants), and creating a business model that is focused on the neutrality of operation and network growth. This valuation consideration should be the focus of the MVE, which becomes a testbed to prove ecosystem sustainability and an input into the model promoting sustainable and continual growth of the network. The network growth can be represented by either the diversity of the ecosystem, exponential growth in transaction volumes, or creation of new business synergies due to co-creation elements of interaction between participants.

Ideally, to use MVE to drive subsequent growth in the business network, you must employ the business valuation models. Although some business models might be standardized tools, consider the possibilities for growth and emergence of new business models due to new platforms and interactions. These additional considerations are assumed with the presence of MVE as proof points.

GOVERNANCE AND RISK

Governance and risk are as important investment considerations, just as insurance is in personal finance. Governance models should reflect efficient, accurate, and effective risk monitoring. Effective risk modeling and governance policies are responsible investments that focus on identifying and avoiding risks that can negatively influence investment returns. The blockchain model risk framework (BMRF) defines the model and its appropriate use to derive value from blockchain investment.

GROWTH AND SCALE

Growth implies the addition of resources at the same rate as revenues increase. *Scale* entails adding revenues at a rapid rate while adding resources at an incremental rate. Scale leads to exponential revenue growth, while growth implies incremental or proportional increases in the business. The distinction between the two is as important as the balance between the two strategies. Sustainable growth implies the addition of new ecosystem players, which leads to the emergence of new business models and monetization options from the improved services and business model of the blockchain network, leading to scale. To achieve growth and scale, we must apply business analysis acumen and tools to continually analyze the business patterns and continually innovate to use the business network.

Clearly, it is vital for an enterprise to establish an investment rubric as a risk mitigation technique. This layered abstraction represents both the investment criteria and the broader landscape. Devising a comprehensive investment profile and model is a significant step in communicating to investors, business partners, and stakeholders the extent and depth of analysis, and developing a clear and defensible plan for project execution, deployment, and risk mitigation that is embedded at every layer of the rubric.

RETURN ON INVESTMENT MODELING

The blockchain investment rubric provides a modeling and analysis tool to assess the investment and measure outcomes. ROI modeling can be viewed as a component of the rubric that aids in assessing the profitability of the investment. The ROI measurement is evaluated relative to the cost of the investment. The cost calculations for the capital that is committed can be complex, and the lower layers of the ROI modeling, such as business valuation and the PoC and design component, can aid in the cost of investment calculations.

ROI is a popular financial metric due to its universal applicability to all kinds of investment and capital projects. Although the various ROI models have different approaches and outcomes, ROI modeling in some form is essential to determine the preferred opportunities. ROI model analysis also exposes the risk elements that might impede achievement of the profitability objectives. In addition, it showcases the investment appetite for a project when compared to measurable cost inefficiencies or a potential new business in the blockchain network. Here is an example ROI calculation:

$$\text{ROI} = [(\text{gain from investment} - \text{cost of investment}) / (\text{cost of investment})] / 100$$

Whereas ROI aids in calculating the project's return on investment, capital budgeting is a practice that helps determine the feasibility of investment into a long-term project. Essentially, capital budgeting provides tools that aid in analyzing cash flows and overall return for the life of the project.

Devising a meaningful ROI model for a blockchain-powered business network is a complex business and financial exercise because of the following factors:

1. The blockchain network is an ecosystem that is composed of many participants and ecosystem players. Their access to the ecosystem and network relies on *individual investment priorities and risk appetite.*

2. The blockchain network relies on a sound business model. It usually is not a stand-alone project, but rather is composed of many elements, such as a partnership or consortium structure, partnership funding model, and consortium-driven business model. Collectively, these elements represent a *complex layer of a financial model and a structure of individual founding members.*

3. Blockchain networks are industry-specific, and depending on the industry subsegment, the ROI models depend on the *industry-driven market infrastructure and market economies.*

4. Ecosystems address the industry-led transformation. They aspire to transform by disruption by creating efficiencies that use disintermediation. This transformation leads to emergence of *new business models* that do not have a defined financial, ROI, or risk model or a defined business structure. Most of the ROI analysis is based on assumptions.

5. A blockchain network requires availability of expertise and talent. Lack of a skilled talent pool in a blockchain technology space and lack of foundational understanding and business modeling, financial structures, and business design introduce huge project planning and operational risks for blockchain business networks, which makes ROI modeling a challenge at the beginning of the project idea.

Although the widely used valuation models provide a methodology to assess and make investment decisions, blockchain networks are about ecosystems. They represent an important progression toward disruption and a new and emerging business model. The elements for asset tokenization and the resulting token and instance economy inject an interesting twist into the valuation exercise.

Because these blockchain-based business models depict a future state and rely on network creation as a building block, some of these business models and their accompanying financial models include new assumptions and creative modeling techniques, which require vision and leadership support. The goal of an industry-specific business model must be considered in every blockchain valuation model exercise, as shown in Figure 7.4.

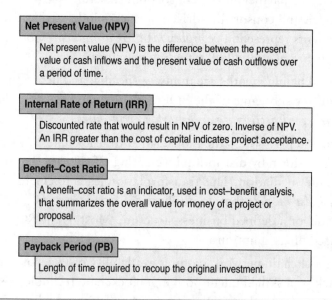

Blockchain Network/Project Valuation Models

Net Present Value (NPV)
Net present value (NPV) is the difference between the present value of cash inflows and the present value of cash outflows over a period of time.

Internal Rate of Return (IRR)
Discounted rate that would result in NPV of zero. Inverse of NPV. An IRR greater than the cost of capital indicates project acceptance.

Benefit–Cost Ratio
A benefit–cost ratio is an indicator, used in cost–benefit analysis, that summarizes the overall value for money of a project or proposal.

Payback Period (PB)
Length of time required to recoup the original investment.

Figure 7.4 Valuation models for a blockchain network.

Some valuation methods used for blockchain projects are discussed next.

NET PRESENT VALUE

Net present value (NPV) is a calculation that compares the amount invested today to the present value of the future cash receipts from the investment—that is, the amount that is invested is compared to the future cash amounts after they are discounted by a specified rate of return.[2]

NPV is a popular tool that focuses on the time value of money (TVM) concept, and ensures that the correct comparisons are made to other projects that are competing for the available investment capital. For a blockchain project, this situation is important due to the risk–reward ratios involved: Those projects that are aimed at transformation are likely to be less attractive due to other competing and more mature technology projects. However, a disruptive element and a focus on a new business stream can potentially make a blockchain project an attractive proposition.

INTERNAL RATE OF RETURN

The internal rate of return (IRR) is the rate at which the project breaks even. According to Knight,[3] it is commonly used by financial analysts with NPV because the two methods are similar but use different variables. With NPV, you assume a discount rate for your company, and then calculate the present value of the investment. With IRR, you calculate the actual return that is provided by the project's cash flows, and then compare this rate of return with your company's hurdle rate (how much it mandates that investments return).[3] By convention, if the IRR is higher than the hurdle rate, it is considered a worthwhile investment. IRR is a conceptual approach that can take into account the issue of growth but not scale. It depends on the subjective interpretation of the decision makers, which might make the investment justification complex and subjective.

BENEFIT–COST RATIO (BCR)

The benefit–cost ratio (BCR) is a financial ratio used to determine whether the amount of money that is made through a project is greater than the costs that are incurred in executing the project. If the costs outweigh the benefits, then the project does not deliver value for money under the assumed conditions.

The BCR has two elements: (1) the benefits of a project or proposal and (2) the costs of the project or proposal. Qualitative factors, such as the benefit a project might have to society, should be expressed in monetary terms where possible to ensure an accurate result.[4]

BCR is an interesting valuation technique for an enterprise because it addresses the transformational elements of the project and the enterprise's readiness for the disruptive side of the equation. When BCR is coupled with NPV to evaluate a project, you can determine the financial justification and assumptions regarding the new business models, and counter disruptive forces by ensuring that the platform and ecosystem readiness represent a long-term benefit.

PAYBACK PERIOD

The payback period (PB) is the length of time required to recover the cost of an investment. It is an important determinant of whether to undertake a position or project because longer payback periods are not wanted for investment positions.

The payback period ignores the TVM, unlike other methods of capital budgeting, such as NPV, IRR, and discounted cash flow.[5] The payback period for blockchain projects might be an inadequate measure of ROI due to technology and inception risks. Because of the time it might take to develop an MVE and to scale the network beyond the MVE, the payback period method does not consider innovation risk and first-market advantage, which is a part of blockchain project framework.

In summary, ROI is a popular financial metric due to its universal applicability to all kinds of investment and capital projects. Devising a meaningful ROI model for a blockchain-powered business network is a complex business and financial exercise. Although these widely used valuation models provide a methodology to assess and make investment decisions, blockchain networks are about ecosystems, and present an important progression toward disruption and new emerging business models. The goal of an industry-specific business model should be a consideration in every blockchain valuation modeling exercise.

RISK MODELING

Risk modeling is about defining a model and quantifying risk, and then devising a model that can classify and profile risk. Taking calculated risk is integral to any new business, and blockchain projects are no different. It might be vital to devise a risk model and simulations to start addressing strategic, operational, compliance, and other types of industry-specific risks. The core idea is to create a robust risk profile and then devise a model to classify and institute risk mitigation strategies, thereby ensuring that the blockchain-powered business network serves the intended business model and can cope with the risk matrix that is imposed by the industry, operating environment, and technology evolution. While many blockchain business networks aim to address a specific industry (or a specific ecosystem within an industry), the network itself is subject to industry-specific risks, blockchain-driven technology risks, and the operational risks of the new ecosystem that a blockchain network aims to create.

Risk modeling seeks to understand the specific risks associated with domains (industry, technology, operations, and others) and to devise a model that can evaluate the impacts to the entire system. These impacts might be financial, reputational, or systemic. The creation of a risk model requires a simulation exercise that tests the proposed models and is used to devise a risk mitigation plan.

Perhaps you want to understand threats to your supply chain or evaluate the geopolitical risks of entering an emerging market, or how an adaptive adversary (such as a hacker or terrorist) might attack you. After risk models are developed, they can be used to evaluate not only how a system behaves under normal operating conditions but also under hypothetical "what if" scenarios. This helps organizations determine their level of risk tolerance and evaluate how to build resiliency into systems to be able to withstand various impacts.[6]

Figure 7.5 shows four types of risks considered in a risk model for a blockchain network or project. The presence of layers of risk elements means that to assess systemic risk, we must devise a model risk framework or a blockchain model risk framework (BMRF). A risk model is about understanding the risk matrix and constructing a robust, organic, and effective model that is based on a framework that is effective enough to adapt to changing market conditions, technology landscapes, the dynamic nature of business models, and the resulting financial structure and model of a particular industry segment.

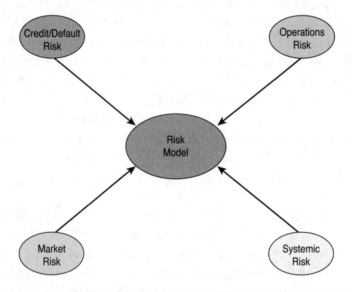

Figure 7.5 Risks evaluated for a blockchain network.

BLOCKCHAIN MODEL RISK FRAMEWORK

All blockchain business networks have a spectrum of risks, such as operational risks, regulatory risks, and financial risks. These business networks must devise a business and operational structure that will enable them to remain profitable and economically viable so as to meet the core objectives of the business entity that operates the network, and to provide the ROI required by the investors and stakeholders. Thus, BMRF acts as a vehicle to devise a mechanism to model, manage, and mitigate risk.

The BMRF discipline is relatively new but essential to providing a wide spectrum of risk analysis and instruments to contain it. At its most basic level, the BMRF defines a methodology to understand the layered risks between various blockchain network operational components and support efforts to manage, mitigate, and reduce those risks.

Although enterprises and projects might use many different risk models, a rapid shift in regulatory frameworks, the rapid evolution of the blockchain technology landscape, the lack of a qualified talent pool, and the emergence of new business models that are attributable to blockchain have prompted many of these enterprises and projects to consider using the BMRF. The idea behind devising a model risk framework is to ensure that risk management satisfies the regulatory elements and captures value effectively and thoroughly.

Within the BMRF, enterprises are prompted to use the right inputs to improve profitability through a reduced cost of compliance and optimized cost reduction, effective capital utilization, and improved operational and process efficiency. Collectively, these factors lead to efficient capture of value from the blockchain network. The value that is captured benefits the network operator as well as the network participants and ecosystem that rely on network efficiency.

The stakes in managing model risk are high. The real test of a risk model framework occurs when things go wrong:

> When things go wrong, consequences can be severe. With digitization and automation, more models are being integrated into business processes, exposing institutions to greater model risk and consequent operational losses. The risk lies equally in defective models and model misuse.[7]

Figure 7.6 presents a comprehensive framework for financial, valuation, and risk models. The elements of the BMRF are discussed next.

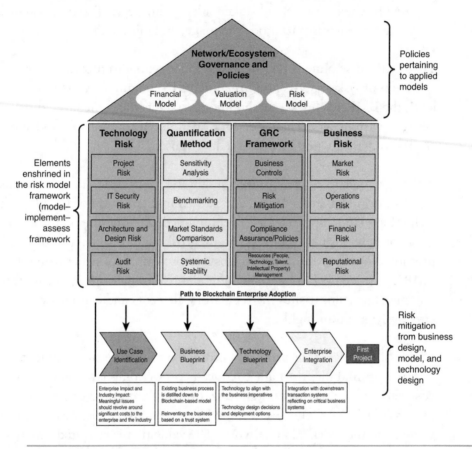

Figure 7.6 Framework for blockchain-based business network risks.

Devising a Business and Technology Blueprint

The idea behind defining the path to blockchain enterprise adoption is to ensure that we have a microscopic focus on a singular use case and that we distill the existing business into a blockchain paradigm. This idea implies the existence of both business and technology models. We take a singular use case that has an industry and enterprise impact and then apply business and technology acumen to the problem domain. The result is a well-thought-out business architecture and technology blueprint that has requirements for compliance, audit, and enterprise integration. The point of this exercise is to use the correct business domain expertise and blockchain technology expertise to derive an adoption model that enlists and surfaces hurdles, challenges, and factors to determine the economic viability of the blockchain solution.

The resulting artifacts and collateral of the blockchain engagement are instrumental in socializing and providing a blueprint for a business that seeks executive sponsorship and the necessary funding for a project. This blueprint should be the first step in use case identification and determining the risk mitigation tool to resolve business commitment challenges.

Technology Risks

Technology risks include choosing the correct technology frameworks, ensuring that our choices adhere to IT risk models, and using open standards that ensure the longevity of technology innovation as well as the availability of talent and usage of technology at a lower cost due to wider participation and adoption from the community and industry. Technology risks can lead to cost overruns in infrastructure planning, maintenance, talent acquisition, and the overall software development costs for the blockchain project. The risk elements include IT security risks, information security risks, massive cost overruns due to poor architecture and design, and talent acquisition challenges due to attrition and access to quality talent.

Quantification Risks

Quantification risks translate the probability and impact of a risk into a measurable quantity. The value or quantum of the risk, in the context of projects, is added to the project cost or time estimate as a contingency value. Project risk quantification and cost and schedule contingency are, therefore, inseparable.[8]

Quantification risks focus on systemic stability, benchmarking (with industry standards), and market standards comparisons. Quantification analysis can be a difficult task, especially the first time that we build a certain kind of project. In such a case, there is no available benchmarking or other project-specific data, which makes this project high risk.

GRC Framework

Governance, risk management, and compliance are three related facets that help assure an organization reliably achieves objectives, addresses uncertainty and acts with integrity.[9]

Lack of business controls, risk mitigation strategies, compliance control and adherence policies, and robust policies concerning intellectual property (IP), talent, and personnel lead to systemic risk due to interdependencies between the various governance frameworks. The cost of compliance (or noncompliance), erroneous risk mitigation strategies, and lack of control procedures regarding IP, talent, and enterprise resources can destabilize the financial model regardless of its operational efficiency.

Business Risks

Business risks imply uncertainty in profits or the danger of loss. Some events might pose a risk due to some unforeseen circumstances in future, which cause the business to fail.[10]

Business risks include market risk, operational risk, financial risk, and systemic risk, which either alone or collectively contribute to the failure of a blockchain-powered business network. Spending time on creating an appropriate business model and business design is an important consideration, along with implementation of a GRC framework and risk modeling.

Blockchain Governance and Policies

Blockchain network operators must implement and define a governance structure with policies for the various models. The policy framework may be network-wide or pertain to a specific model, such as an ROI, financial, or risk model. The policies provide guidelines for dealing with model risks and create a landscape for performing analysis. Governance policies can be the first line of defense when dealing with model risks, or they can be an impediment to network operations and growth. It is vital to consider the balance between managing risk and restricting the environment in terms of growth vectors.

Risk modeling is about defining a model and quantifying risk, and then devising a model that can classify and profile that risk. It requires understanding the various domains' specific risks and evaluating their potential impacts—financial, reputational, or systemic—on the entire system. The presence of layered risk elements implies that to assess systemic risk we might need to devise a model risk framework or BMRF. The BMRF encourages us to use the right inputs to improve profitability through a reduced cost of compliance and optimized cost reduction, effective capital utilization, and improved operational and process efficiency, all of which lead to efficient capture of value from the blockchain network.

CHAPTER SUMMARY

Although many blockchain projects and networks are emerging, challenges remain in regard to addressing the technical complexity of the blockchain protocol and navigating the sea of available frameworks that claim that they can solve industry-specific inefficiencies. A key challenge is defining standards by using a framework that aims to shape the meaningful and scalable usage of blockchain technology. Despite the technology adoption challenges involved in making blockchain work for businesses, blockchain's ability to transform businesses by creating a global platform that enables trust among participants has the potential to surpass the transformational power of the Internet.

The goal is to create a trusted digital transaction network that facilitates the exchange of value without any agency or human monitoring, control, and intermediation. This powerful concept has immense business implications.

Although enterprises, industries, and the ecosystem understand this potential, the transformative and disruptive elements of a blockchain-powered business network and the lack of proven business and financial design, frameworks, and modeling are currently hindering the industrial adoption of blockchain.

Industries, consortia, and enterprises must understand and devise a framework and a model that take into account the various valuation models, financial and business structures, risk models, and governance frameworks to ensure a methodical, quantifiable, and measurable deployment of resources while effectively managing risk. These frameworks should aim to identify value by pragmatically assessing the impact, feasibility, risk, and technology deployment with granularity, and then focus on the various levels of investment, risk, governance, and ROIs with an industry- and subsector-level focus.

The model framework should aim to capture value by molding the strategic intent through an economically viable deployment of technology to shape the business network, ecosystem, and digital marketplace while addressing regulatory and compliance barriers. With the correct mixture of strategic approach, business design, financial rubric, GRC framework, and access to technology acumen and talent, a blockchain-powered business network can transform industries and businesses while being disruptive and immensely profitable.

REFERENCES

1. "Emerging Technology Projection: The Total Economic Impact of IBM Blockchain—Projected Cost Savings and Business Benefits Enabled by IBM Blockchain." www-01.ibm.com/common/ssi/cgi-bin/ssialias?htmlfid=79017679USEN.

2. www.accountingcoach.com/blog/npv-net-present-value

3. hbr.org/2016/03/a-refresher-on-internal-rate-of-return

4. bizfluent.com/how-6200049-calculate-benefit-cost-ratio.html

5. www.investopedia.com/terms/p/paybackperiod.asp

6. www2.deloitte.com/mn/en/pages/governance-risk-and-compliance/articles/risk-modeling.html

7. www.mckinsey.com/business-functions/risk/our-insights/the-evolution-of-model-risk-management

8. www.pmi.org/learning/library/quantitative-risk-assessment-methods-9929

9. go.oceg.org/grc-capability-model-red-book

10. www.investopedia.com/terms/b/businessrisk.asp#axzz27Teb1xOk

8

LOOKING AHEAD: WHAT DOES THE FUTURE HOLD?

Blockchain is here … for good.

—Jerry Cuomo

Reading up to this point, we hope you are eager to help your organization become a blockchain business. With blockchain, we can reimagine many of the world's most fundamental business processes and open the door to new styles of digital interactions that we have yet to imagine. Today, blockchain is fulfilling its potential of vastly reducing the cost and complexity of getting things done across industries and government. Blockchain is certainly here for good. The term "for good" has a double meaning: It implies that blockchain is not a passing fad, and it suggests that blockchain is providing a foundation of trust that is delivering a social good—namely, significantly reducing the various pestilences afflicting digital business, including counterfeiting, digital surveillance, and identity theft.

So far, we have seen only the beginning of blockchain's transformative power for business. As we look ahead to the future, we will see blockchain effects multiply. Specifically, networks will come together in a way that unlocks their power across ecosystems and industries, unleashing the "network of network" effect. We will also see blockchain at the nexus of emerging technologies like artificial intelligence (AI), the Internet of Things (IoT), and quantum computing. In these cases, blockchain will accelerate the adoption of these technologies by adding the missing element of trust, while also benefiting from the distinct capabilities that these technologies deliver. In this final chapter, we will examine these dual effects.

THE NETWORK OF NETWORKS

Each day, new live blockchain solutions enter into production. A "live blockchain solution" is a blockchain network with multiple members who are adding blocks and exchanging value on a daily basis. Although these blockchain solutions may be producing value for their own participants, they are isolated. If individual blockchain solutions remain isolated, that scenario begs a question: How many will there be? How many applications/solutions will an organization need to engage with for all the networks to which it belongs? But what if individual blockchain solutions could interoperate? Might they produce even more value if they were connected together?

Looking beyond today's implementations, we see a future in which blockchain technologies enable a network of networks, creating additional value and further reimagining the way economies, governments, corporations, and more work together. A blockchain economy emerges when an organization's blockchain network is represented by a "web" of interconnected networks. This kind of intertwined architecture would allow an organization to connect and transact with multiple solutions, going beyond the bounds of a single network, and opening up a market of interoperability across solutions. Essentially, an organization could have one application or entry point and one peer (ledger), instead of multiple iterations of these elements, to engage with every network and solution that is relevant to its business.

To put the potential impact of a blockchain network of networks into perspective, let's look at an example involving a fictional company called Global Produce Supply (GPS). GPS is a produce distribution and whole-sale business. For GPS to be successful when engaging with its end customers and partners, the company must ensure the safety and quality of its produce, streamline its shipping/distribution processes, and make and receive timely payments vis-à-vis its partners. To help meet these expectations, GPS has joined three different blockchain networks—one for food quality and safety, one for shipping, and one for trade financing. Each of these blockchain solutions is individually bringing value to GPS, but they are disparate entities and do not have the capability to interoperate.

Or do they? Think about the value that could be created by connecting and interoperating these networks, forming GPS's network of networks. The company could use one solution (made up of all three networks) to ensure the quality and safety of its produce; bring trust, traceability, and transparency to the associated shipment process; and use the trade finance network to conduct financial transactions with its partners. This would potentially create an additional layer of value on top of the existing value already created by blockchain.

Today, individual blockchain solutions are changing industries in unprecedented ways. When blockchain networks and solutions begin to interoperate as suggested in the GPS example, however, they could unlock additional value beyond the capabilities of today's networks.

On September 14, 2018, IBM and HACERA took one of the first—but necessary—steps toward achieving this objective. IBM joined HACERA's Unbounded Registry, which serves as a sort of "yellow pages" directory, enabling companies to discover and participate in existing blockchain networks and solutions.[1] Available networks and solutions listed in the registry are built on a variety of blockchain frameworks, including Hyperledger Fabric, Ethereum Quorum, R3 Corda, Stellar, and more. The registry continues to add to its growing base of participants, including vendors such as IBM, Oracle, Microsoft, and consortia and developers from all around the globe. We are so happy that the Unbounded Registry is helping more participants to collaborate openly, through permissioned and nonpermissioned blockchains. We keep encouraging blockchain participants to join, get listed, and collaborate using this registry.

The next step in this process is to continue unlocking the power of existing blockchain technologies and begin to interconnect or layer them in a multilingual manner. To maximize value from blockchain solutions, each organization should consider how its individual blockchain solutions might be interconnected. Fortunately, we don't have to reinvent the wheel.

Let's consider how this is possible with blockchain technology today; more specifically, let's look at Hyperledger Fabric–based networks. We think the peer and channel components of a Fabric network are where the true power of a network of networks can be realized. The peer is where distributed ledgers reside, while the channels are private sub-networks between members. Organizations might potentially use their peer to connect into multiple blockchain networks via channels, thereby unlocking the power of the peer. This significantly reduces the complexity and optimizes an organization's interactions with different blockchain networks.

In addition to taking full advantage of the power of the Fabric peer, we can begin embedding multilingual smart contract capabilities in existing blockchain technologies. Notably, some blockchain frameworks have modular architectures, which enable them to support a wide variety of languages for writing smart contracts. For example, networks built on Hyperledger Fabric have the ability to use Ethereum (EVM/Solidity) smart contracts. Therefore, a solution containing smart contracts written in Solidity can be available to users of these networks. These capabilities will continue to evolve, especially since the partnership announcement made by Hyperledger and the Enterprise Ethereum Alliance on October 1, 2018.[2] This collaboration represents a major step forward for the entire blockchain community.

Finally, the component that will bring these blockchain networks and solutions together for an organization is a mash-up application. This is expected to profoundly change the way organizations engage with blockchain networks and solutions by requiring them to interact with just one consistent application programming interface (API), rather than an API for every network. This mash-up application can include a variety of capabilities defined in data models and smart contracts, but at a fundamental level it will serve as the glue that joins various networks together. As an organization continues to expand its use of blockchain, this architecture will allow the enterprise to scale accordingly and innovate at speeds necessary for competing successfully in its industry. Much like cloud platforms have delivered value for application development, blockchain platforms—such as the IBM Blockchain Platform—will facilitate the advancement and delivery of these blockchain mash-up applications.

Organizations plus solutions are where networks form. Today, we are seeing first-order benefits, but many solutions remain siloed. Even so, we are edging closer to a tomorrow where an organization's ability to interconnect solutions does not restrict the organization and its solutions to a single network. We realized from the start that you cannot do blockchain on your own: You need a vibrant community and ecosystem of like-minded innovators who share the vision of helping to transform the way companies conduct business in the global economy. Blockchain technology is just beginning to scratch the surface of its potential; however, if we design blockchain frameworks and solutions to interconnect, we can unlock the full power of a blockchain network of networks—thereby forming the blockchain economy.

BLOCKCHAIN AT THE NEXUS OF TECHNOLOGY

Blockchain stands to accelerate the adoption of emerging technologies including AI, cloud, and IoT by bringing in the missing element of trust, which is required for business to fully embrace these technologies at scale. On the flip side, blockchain business networks stand to benefit from the integration of these technologies into modern blockchain platforms and applications.

BLOCKCHAIN AND ARTIFICIAL INTELLIGENCE

Blockchain and AI are on just about every chief information officer's watch list of game-changing technologies that stand to reshape industries. Both technologies come with immense benefits, but both also bring their own challenges for adoption. It is also fair to say that the hype surrounding these technologies individually may be unprecedented, so the thought of bringing these two ingredients together may be viewed by some as brewing a modern-day version of IT pixie dust. At the same time, there is a logical way to think about this mash-up that is both sensible and pragmatic.

Today, AI is for all intents and purposes a centralized process. An end user must have extreme faith in the central authority to produce a trusted business outcome. By decentralizing the three key elements of AI—that is, data, models, and analytics—blockchain can deliver the trust and confidence often needed for end users to fully adopt and rely on AI-based business processes.

Let's explore how blockchain is poised to enrich AI by bringing trust to data, models, and analytics.

Your Data Is Your Data

Many of the world's most notable AI technology services are centralized—including Amazon, Apple, Facebook, Google, and IBM, as well as Chinese companies Alibaba, Baidu, and Tencent. Yet all have encountered challenges in establishing trust among their eager, but somewhat cautious users. How can a business provide assurance to its users that its AI has not overstepped its bounds?

Imagine if these AI services could produce a "forensic report," verified by a third party, to prove to you, beyond a reasonable doubt, how and when businesses are using your data once those are ingested. Imagine further that your data could be used only if you gave permission to do so.

A blockchain ledger can be used as a digital rights management system, allowing your data to be "licensed" to the AI provider under your terms, conditions, and duration. The ledger would act as an access management system storing the proofs and permission by which a business can access and use the user's data.

Trusted AI Models

Consider the example of using blockchain technology as a means of providing trusted data and provenance of training models for machine learning. In this case, we've created a fictitious system to answer the question of whether a fruit is an apple or orange.

This question-answering system that we build is called a "model," and this model is created via a process called "training." The goal of training is to create an accurate model that answers our questions correctly most of the time. Of course, to train a model, we need to collect data to train on—for this example, that could be the color of the fruit (as a wavelength of light) and the sugar content (as a percentage). With blockchain, you can track the provenance of the training data as well as see an audit trail of the evidence that led to the prediction of why a particular fruit is considered an apple versus an orange. A business can also prove that it is not "juicing up" its books by tagging fruit more often as apples, if that is the more expensive of the two fruits.

Explaining AI Decisions

The European Union has adopted a law requiring that any decision made by a machine be readily explainable, on penalty of fines that could cost companies billions of dollars. The EU General Data Protection Regulation (GDPR), which came into force in 2018, includes a right to obtain an explanation of decisions made by algorithms and a right to opt out of some algorithmic decisions altogether.

Massive amounts of data are being produced every second—more data than humans have the ability to assess and use as the basis for drawing conclusions. However, AI applications are capable of assessing large data sets and many variables, while learning about or connecting those variables relevant to its tasks and objectives. For this very reason, AI continues to be adopted in various industries and applications, and we are relying more and more on their outcomes. It is essential, however, that any decisions made by AI are still verified for accuracy by humans. Blockchain can help clarify the provenance, transparency, understanding, and explanations of those outcomes and decisions. If decisions and associated data points are recorded via transactions on a blockchain, the inherent attributes of blockchain will make auditing them much simpler. Blockchain is a key technology that brings trust to transactions in a network; therefore, infusing blockchain into AI decision-making processes could be the element needed to achieve the transparency necessary to fully trust the decisions and outcomes derived from AI.[3]

BLOCKCHAIN AND THE INTERNET OF THINGS

More than a billion intelligent, connected devices are already part of today's IoT. The expected proliferation of hundreds of billions more places us at the threshold of a transformation sweeping across the electronics industry and many other areas.

With the advancement in IoT, industries are now enabled to capture data, gain insight from the data, and make decisions based on the data. Therefore, there is a lot of "trust" in the information obtained. But the real truth of the matter is, do we really know where these data came from? And should we be making decisions and transacting based on data we cannot validate?

For example, did weather data really originate from a censor in the Atlantic Ocean? Or did the shipping container really not exceed the agreed temperature limit? The IoT use cases are massive, but they all share the same issue with trust.

IoT with blockchain can bring real trust to captured data. The underlying idea is to give devices, at the time of their creation, an identity that can be validated and verified throughout their life cycle with blockchain. There is great potential for IoT systems in blockchain technology capabilities that rely on device identity protocols and reputation systems. With a device identity protocol, each device can have its own blockchain public key and send encrypted challenge and response messages to other devices, thereby ensuring a device remains in control of its identity. In addition, a device with an identity can develop a reputation or history that is tracked by a blockchain.[4]

Smart contracts represent the business logic of a blockchain network. When a transaction is proposed, these smart contracts are autonomously executed within the guidelines set by the network. In IoT networks, smart contracts can play a pivotal role by providing automated coordination and authorization for transactions and interactions. The original idea behind IoT was to surface data and gain actionable insight at the right time. For example, smart homes are a thing of the present and most everything can be connected. In fact, with IoT, when something goes wrong, these IoT devices can even take action—for example, ordering a new part. We need a way to govern the actions taken by these devices, and smart contracts are a great way to do so.[5]

In an ongoing experiment in Brooklyn, New York, a community[6] is using a blockchain[7] to record the production of solar energy and enable the purchase of excess renewable energy credits. The device itself has an identity and builds a reputation through its history of records and exchange. Through the blockchain, people can aggregate their purchasing power more easily, share the burden of maintenance, and trust that devices are recording actual solar production.

As IoT continues to evolve and its adoption continues to grow, the ability to autonomously manage devices and actions taken by devices will be essential. Blockchain and smart contracts are positioned well to integrate those capabilities into IoT.

BLOCKCHAIN AND QUANTUM COMPUTING

Blockchain is revolutionizing transactions and business networks through its trust, transparency, and security aspects. Quantum computing will revolutionize compute power to an extent that the digital age has never seen before. But what do the two have in common?

Blockchain is often touted as a technology that is tamper-proof—or at the very least, tamper-resistant. Primarily, this sentiment stems from its reliance on standard cryptographic functions and consensus protocols that guarantee the security of a blockchain. These are relatively secure because breaking them requires huge computing resources, which are not generally available today. And yet the highly touted security of blockchain may have an Achilles' heel: It will be child's play for powerful quantum computers to break the kinds of cryptographic protection implemented in existing, conventional blockchain frameworks.

While quantum computers can disrupt blockchain as it exists now, quantum cybersecurity can also provide a solution. Idalia Friedson, quantum computing expert and co-founder of the Hudson Quantum Initiative, suggests that incorporating emerging quantum cybersecurity in three steps can "save blockchain from the fate of other systems made obsolete by new technologies":

Step 1 involves strengthening existing encryption algorithms by adding in truly random numbers, or so-called quantum keys. Adding quantum keys to blockchain software will provide added security against both a classical computer and a quantum computer.

Step 2 involves developing quantum-resistant algorithms. The U.S. National Institute of Standards and Technology is currently reviewing submissions for these next-generation algorithms. One example, called Lattice cryptography, mathematically has been proven to be resistant to quantum computing attacks. So far, no known algorithms can break this method of encoding data.

Step 3 involves using quantum key distribution hardware to send information from one point to another by encoding data on individual particles. Any attempted hack automatically severs the connection.

The threat posed by quantum computing to blockchain security can be serious, but approaches such as Friedson's three-step plan to develop and implement quantum keys, quantum-resistant algorithms, and quantum key hardware hold promise for thwarting these challenges. With a little forward thinking today, blockchain can continue to provide the foundation of trust through a tamper-resistant ledger and turn around the threat of quantum computing to actually enhance security to even greater levels.

As you can see, blockchain stands to accelerate the adoption of emerging technologies including AI and IoT by bringing in the missing element of trust. Similarly, blockchain business networks stand to benefit from the integration of these technologies into modern blockchain platforms and applications.

We have only just begun to witness blockchain's transformative power for business. As we look ahead to the future, we will almost certainly see blockchain effects multiply.

BLOCKCHAIN OPPORTUNITIES AND CHALLENGES: WHAT LIES AHEAD?

Each chapter in this book was carefully chosen to ensure that business leaders are equipped to use the right content at the right level of depth and meaningfully address the broader conversation (technology funda-mentals and business models) and implementation necessary for the blockchain-based business and technology design for their project. As practitioners, thought leaders, and business leaders, we relied on our expe-riences as we reflected upon the challenges of blockchain project progres-sion, production readiness from the perspectives of both industry and specific businesses, and the technology acumen needed to devise a core blockchain (extensible) network design that lays the foundation of the multiparty transaction network with built-in trust. The severe shortage of technology skills, business model leadership, blockchain system design experience, industry-specific blockchain taxonomy, business model frame-works, risk and investment models, and common business design patterns has been our primary motivation in writing this book.

As active members of the blockchain community, industry groups, block-chain technology standards bodies, and thought leaders, we believe that some complex technical issues still remain to be solved, such as privacy, confidentiality, scalability, and a network-centric approach to code and infrastructure management. Ideally, the resolution of these challenges will lead to an economically viable solution with predictable transaction costs. These complex technical issues have a direct impact on the business design of a decentralized or a quasi-decentralized blockchain-powered business network that provides a platform that facilitates co-creation of new value. Ultimately, the business model that runs the business network depends on cost predictability, economic viability, and new value creation, which in turn are based on the emergence of new business models that are amplified by flattened network processing of transactions.

The thematic elements of this book help ensure a cohesive understanding of technology fundamentals and landscapes, business models, governance and risk structuring, and financial models, which sharpen your decision-making criteria. A sound decision-making process can include various financial, market-driven, and industry-specific data that might impact the quality of your decision. The frameworks and rubrics that we present can help you institute a simple, quantifiable, and peer-accepted model that facilitates decision making.

Our experiences led us to include the chapters that discuss risk modeling, risk model frameworks, and project financial models. We provide a framework that enables business leaders to take a methodical approach to understand and quantify risk, which includes the full spectrum of technology risks, compliance risks, and industry-specific risks. Our risk model framework treats risk as an opportunity rather than a limiting factor. This framework focuses on sharing of risk among blockchain members and the resulting opportunity to add to the bottom line, which injects a new perspective into project financial modeling and traditional approaches to governance, risk, and compliance (GRC) frameworks.

You must understand industry-specific innovation and adoption patterns to ensure your organization's readiness for participating in production-grade, blockchain-powered business networks. We describe the trust divide in the technology landscape section to address the foundation and technology landscape that influences the business models for a chosen use case, which can be a subsegment of an industry. Chapters 3 and 4 provide a solid foundation of technology fundamentals and reveal their lasting impact on business models. The choice matrix we suggest can help business leaders select the best choice of architecture that results from the business design and solution design activities. The investment rubrics we delineate will arm business leaders with a framework to ensure wise and judicious use of enterprise resources, and our proposed risk mitigation tool is intended to ensure that the investment yields milestone objectives at every stage of the project.

Linking technology fundamentals to business models, we take a technology-neutral approach to deciding between permissioned and permissionless networks. To understand the trust divide between these types of networks is to understand the divide between enterprise-driven blockchain technologies, which are inclined toward permissioned blockchain and primarily transformative, and the crypto asset–driven world, which is permissionless and largely in the public blockchain domain, acting as a disruptor to every industry that aspires to employ blockchain to transform and reinvent its operations. Regardless of which side you choose, it is vital for you to employ the tools and frameworks described in this book to understand and classify the motivation and technology advancement of both sides; ultimately, the innovation and resulting reinvention of business models that ensues will lead to new economic values that will change the world.

Beyond the scope and context of the topics covered in this book, it is vital to understand that gaps, inefficiencies, and other limiting aspects of the current centrally managed world versus the complete decentralization of every aspect of business transaction fall along a spectrum. From all our engagements, we have realized that the acceptable path to disruption lies somewhere in between the two extremes, as industries adopt a new model that coexists with their current (centralized) systems. Moving to a completely decentralized or quasi-decentralized model must be a gradual process to mitigate risk and account for the cultural elements of a business network. The path to complete decentralization is not an easy one. The transformational projects in the forms of proofs of concept and pilots that are undertaken by industry leaders and consortia represent an effort to understand the technology, trust, and transactions risks before they transition to a fully decentralized world. The spectrum from centralized to completely decentralized is an interesting one, and innovation is incubating on both sides of the camp.

We hope that this book has been an interesting, informative, and educational journey regarding the business adoption challenges for blockchain technology projects and the overall business perspective regarding the challenges and adoption guidelines. This project has been an interesting one for us because of the rapid pace of changes and evolution in the blockchain technology landscape. The emerging business models and the promise of industry-wide transformation create an exciting arena that is both purposeful and a constant source of energy—which in turn keeps us motivated to continue on the path to understanding the potential of the blockchain technology by innovating and applying that innovation to address the disruption and transformation of industries. This book provides the basics needed for a strong business model foundation and deeper insights into some of the core elements of blockchain business design and its business blueprint.

OVERALL SUMMARY

In this book, you learned all that you need to know to start building a successful blockchain network. As you begin building your blockchain, it is useful to reflect on what you learned from each chapter and what the future might hold.

Chapter 2, "Opportunities and Challenges," provided an overview of the opportunities that blockchain offers, and the challenges that you must consider to benefit from those opportunities. Blockchain is transformative, presenting new opportunities such as a distributed organizational structure, a trusted business model, and a decentralized ecosystem. Many industries can take advantage of these opportunities, such as banking and financial markets, insurance, healthcare, retail and consumer goods, government, media and entertainment, automotive, and travel and transportation. But with these opportunities come a set of challenges, which include setting the scope of your blockchain network, gathering and using the motivation to build the network, setting up a governance structure to manage the network, and obtaining the technology to make it work on the ground. Although blockchain is a disruptive technology that requires adapting your business as blockchain changes the industry landscape, with the correct scope, motivation, and governance structures in place, you can ride the wave of this changing landscape and do more than survive: You can prosper and gain a competitive advantage in your markets.

You have seen the opportunities and challenges involved in creating a blockchain network, but what is the actual landscape in which you are building that network? Chapter 3, "Understanding the Technology Landscape," explored the lay of the land and described the environment and technical aspects you can expect to address. In an enterprise blockchain network, you use a permissioned network to ensure that only the people whom you want to be involved in the blockchain network can access it. Chapter 3 also discussed the costs of building the network, which has a superb return on investment if it is correctly implemented, and its expected longevity. Most importantly, you learned about the crypto assets (tokens) that your blockchain generates and ultimately derives value from. These assets must be protected and used to grow the network, which then generates ever-increasing value.

This topic is a critical one to understand. You must have an excellent grasp of all the technical aspects of a blockchain network to ensure that it can easily and quickly adapt to the disruptive forces that it brings. A solid technical base ensures a solid blockchain as it evolves.

To get the most of out of your enterprise blockchain network, you must pick the correct business and technology model for your business and industry. You will want to use a model that provides the most economic incentives to join a blockchain, such as creating more value with the network than you can produce alone, and is best suited to your business and industry. The correct model will also ease the transition into a blockchain network and allow you to take the greatest advantage of blockchain's disruptive aspects. Among the many possible business models are the joint venture, consortium, new company (NewCo), business ecosystem, build–own–operate (BOO) or founder-led networks, and build–own–operate–transfer (BOOT) or founding consortium networks. All this information and more was described in Chapter 4, "Business of Business Models."

Next to understanding the technology of blockchain, selecting the model is perhaps the most important decision that you will make in implementing your blockchain. A model that is well suited to your business and industry will be easier to implement and provide the best return on investment (ROI). Conversely, an ill-suited model not only will not produce value, but can actually decrease value. Thus, it is imperative that you find the right fit for the right business.

At this point, you should have a model for your blockchain network and be ready to implement it. The first thing that you need to do is set up a governance structure, which ensures that you and your ecosystem partners have a common vision and goals for the blockchain network. With a governance structure in place, the ecosystem partners will know how their blockchain network is managed. Chapter 5, "Developing a Governance Structure for Blockchain Networks," described how to set up the governance structure, which addresses industry-specific requirements and ensures a tight linkage between the business model and the technology blueprint. By adopting a common governance structure, all participants adhere to a common set of objectives, fair and equitable use of network resources, and rules of engagement.

Governance ensures that your blockchain network runs smoothly and efficiently and produces the most value. A good governance structure can mean the difference between a mediocre blockchain network and a dominant and profitable one. Thus, in addition to having the correct technology and model for your blockchain, you must have an infrastructure that governs it well.

Creating a blockchain is not a solo effort! To build a successful blockchain, you must gather a team of experts who take on various duties and roles in the creation of the network. You need an enterprise-level team that consists of high-level roles, such as founders, members, operators, and users of the network. Then, you need the folks who are in the trenches and have their hands deeply involved in building the network, such as steering committee members, project managers, blockchain consultants, engineers, and many more roles. All these experts work together by using the concept of interprise synergy, in which each expert is empowered to work as a decentralized authority with a great deal of autonomy within the larger network. Chapter 6, "Building a Team to Drive Blockchain Projects," described these team members and their roles.

As with picking the correct technology, model, and governance structure, you need to pick the correct people for each role that is part of building a blockchain. Each team member should be an expert in his or her field and have the autonomy and authority to make decisions within the confines of his or her role, but no more. You do not want a team member to come up against another role and disrupt or damage the work of that role.

In the course of reading this book, you learned that many challenges surround the technical complexity of blockchain. One such challenge is the plethora of financial models, investment rubrics, and frameworks (structures that aim to scale blockchain networks with the greatest efficiency) available today. Which do you choose? Chapter 7, "Understanding Financial Models, Investment Rubrics, and Model Risk Frameworks," provided guidance for deciding which elements are best for your network. Its lessons can help ensure a methodical, quantifiable, and measurable deployment of resources while effectively managing risk, all at scale. With the correct mixture of a strategic approach, business design, financial rubric, GRC frameworks, and access to technology acumen and correct talent, a blockchain-powered business network can transform industries and businesses while being disruptive and immensely profitable.

It's difficult to manage risk while ensuring the best deployment of your resources if you do not use the correct tools. As you build and implement your blockchain network, you must ensure that your financial models, investment rubrics, and risk frameworks provide the best risk and reward ratio for your business and your industry. Think carefully about which tools to use.

Building a blockchain network is not an easy task, but if you use the knowledge that you gained from reading this book, you can produce a network that can produce social good, facilitate cooperation among businesses and industries that benefit all the participants, and generate immense value for your business. Now is the time to take advantage of this new and radical technology that will change the business landscape for many years to come.

REFERENCES

1. Cuomo, Jerry. "The Yellow Pages of Blockchain Has Arrived: Networks Are Now Visible to the World." *Blockchain Unleashed: IBM Blockchain Blog.* IBM Blockchain, 2018. www.ibm.com/blogs/blockchain/2018/09/the-yellow-pages-of-blockchain-has-arrived-networks-are-now-visible-to-the-world/.

2. Murphy, Colby. "Joining Forces for the Advancement of Blockchain Technologies." *Blockchain Unleashed: IBM Blockchain Blog.* IBM Blockchain,

2018. www.ibm.com/blogs/blockchain/2018/10/joining-forces-for-the-advancement-of-blockchain-technologies/.

3. Modex Team. "Combining Blockchain and Artificial Intelligence for a Better Future." *Blog.modex.tech*, August 13, 2018. blog.modex.tech/combining-blockchain-and-artificial-intelligence-for-a-better-future-421e97141e60.

4. Lombardo, Hans. "Blockchain Serves as Tool for Human, Product and IoT Device Identity Validation." *Chain of Things*. Chain of Things Limited, January 11, 2017. www.chainofthings.com/news/2017/1/11/blockchain-serves-as-tool-for-human-product-and-iot-device-identity-validation.

5. Smartz. "How Blockchain and Smart Contracts Can Impact IoT." *Smartz Platform Blog: Medium*, August 21, 2018. medium.com/smartz-blog/how-blockchain-and-smart-contracts-can-impact-iot-f9e77ebe02ab.

6. "The Future of Energy Is Local." *Brooklynmicrogrid.com*. Brooklyn Microgrid, 2018. brooklynmicrogrid.com/.

7. "The Future of Energy: Blockchain, Transactive Grids, Microgrids, Energy Trading: LO3 Stock, Tokens and Information." LO3 Energy, 2018. lo3energy.com/.

INDEX

A

Access control, digital identity verification for, 30
Accountability
    applying blockchain to f2ood industry, 5
    attributes of enterprise blockchain, 3
Accounting, making blockchain consumable,
    55–56
Advertising, blockchain opportunities, 36–37
AIG, 31
Airbnb, 27
Airlines, blockchain opportunities, 39
Architecture, token evaluation model and, 76–77
Artificial intelligence (AI)
    blockchain preventing counterfeiting, 12
    overview of, 167–168
    securing personal data, 168
    transparency of decision making, 169–170
    trusted models, 169
Asset bridging, exchange mechanisms, 78
Asset/land registration, example of distributed
    ecosystems, 29
Asset-pair trading, monetization strategies, 139
Assets
    assumptions underlying enterprise blockchain
        infrastructure, 81
    crypto assets, 73–74
    exchange mechanisms, 78–79
    government registration of, 35
    token evaluation model, 76–77
    tokens. *See* Tokenization

Auditing, making blockchain consumable, 55
Authentication, making blockchain
    consumable, 55
Authorization, making blockchain consumable, 55
Automation of business processes,
    using smart contracts, 24
Automotive industry, blockchain opportunities,
    37–38
The Autonomous Car, 6

B

B2B (Business-to-business), permissioned
    blockchain and, 58
Banking and financial markets, blockchain
    opportunities, 29
Benefit-cost ratio (BCR)
    business valuation techniques, 144
    overview of, 151–152
    valuation models for blockchain
        network, 150
BFT (Byzantine Fault Tolerant) consensus
    model, 54
Bitcoin
    blockchain compared with, 1
    governance mechanisms, 107
    permissionless blockchain and, 58
    unregulated rogue nature of, 52
BitTorrent, 125
Blockchain architects, project team roles, 131

Blockchain business networks. *See also* Networks
    business network governance, 114–117, 119
    governance disciplines, 109–110
    network infrastructure governance, 120–121
    network membership governance, 112–114, 120
    SCTrustNet governance structure, 118
    technology infrastructure governance, 110–112
Blockchain consultants, project team roles, 130
Blockchain developers, project team roles, 131
Blockchain economy, 164–167
Blockchain introduction
    benefits, 4–5
    connecting social benefit and business
        benefit, 9–12
    core beliefs, 2–3
    dream large, act incrementally, 6–7
    enterprise blockchain, 3–4
    governance, 8
    motivating network members, 7–8
    overview of, 1–2
    questions from business and technology
        leaders, 12–16
    references, 17–18
    summary, 16–17
    trailblazer implementations, 5–6
    types of blockchain, 59
Blockchain investment rubric. *See* Investment rubric
Blockchain model risk framework (BMRF)
    investment and, 147
overview of, 154–156
    risk modeling, 159
Blockchain technology solution team, 134
BSSs (Business support services), 112
Build-Own-Operate (BOO)
    business models for permissioned blockchain,
        96–97
    overview of, 100–101
    table summarizing, 103
Build-Own-Operate-Transfer (BOOT)
    business models for permissioned blockchain,
        96–97
    overview of, 101
    table summarizing, 103
Business
    business-driven solutions, 6–7
    devising business and technology blueprints,
        156–157
    devising business blueprint for blockchain
        model, 90–91
    risk modeling, 158
    separating business domain from supporting
        technology, 63–65

token evaluation model applied to solutions,
    76–77
    valuation, 144, 146–147
    when to use blockchain, 63–65
Business case. *See also* Monetization strategy, 137
Business development manager, project team
    roles, 132
Business ecosystem
    business models for permissioned blockchain,
        96–97
    overview of, 99–100
    table summarizing, 103
Business functions, in enterprise blockchain
    infrastructure, 81
Business good, connecting social benefit with,
    9–12
Business integration, high-level technology
    issues, 62
Business language, in enterprise blockchain
    infrastructure, 81
Business models. *See also* Monetization strategy
    Build-Own-Operate (BOO), 100–101, 103
    Build-Own-Operate-Transfer (BOOT), 101, 103
    business ecosystem, 99–100, 103
    challenges of adopting enterprise blockchain, 50
    comparing permissioned and permissionless
        blockchain, 58
    considerations for, 94–97
    consortium, 98–99, 102
    design and, 92–94
    devising business blueprint, 90–91
    devising technology blueprint, 91–92
    elements required for enterprise blockchain
        maturity, 67
    governance mechanisms, 107
    identifying appropriate use case, 89–90
    integration with existing systems, 92
    joint venture (JV), 98, 102
    minimal viable ecosystem (MVE), 144
    network extensibility and, 84
    NewCo spin-off, 99, 102
    steps in adopting blockchain, 88–89
    summary, 104
    tokenization and, 138
    trusted business model, 27–28
    types of blockchain initiatives, 140
Business network governance
    basic tenets, 115–116
    checklist, 116
    overview of, 114–115
    SCTrustNet governance structure, 119
Business objectives, assessing applicability of
    blockchain, 13

Business rules. *See also* Smart contracts, 52–53
Business structure. *See also* Infrastructure;
    Organizational structure
  business network governance and, 116
  financial modeling and, 141
Business support services (BSSs), 112
Business-to-business (B2B), permissioned
    blockchain and, 58
Byrne, Preston, 72
Byzantine Fault Tolerant (BFT) consensus model, 54

C

Cargo handling, blockchain opportunities, 40
Cars, blockchain opportunities, 37–38
Centralization
  exchange mechanisms, 78
  intraprise synergy and, 133
  limitations of, 26
  organizational structure and, 124
  security of personal data and, 168
Chain decision matrix, when to use blockchain,
    62–63
Chaincode. *See also* Smart contracts
  blockchain technical building blocks, 52–53
  designing business models and, 93
Challenges
  future of blockchain and, 173–176
  governance as, 43–44
  motivation as, 42–43
  overview of, 40–41
  references, 47–48
  scope as, 41–42
  summary, 47
  technology as, 45–47
China UnionPay loyalty program, 37
Clinical trials management, blockchain
    opportunities, 32–33
CLS Group, 5
Co-creation, network governance and, 115
Co-existence, blockchain with existing systems.
    See also Integration, 82
Commerce
  advertising supply chain management, 36–37
  blockchain opportunities, 33–34
  loyalty programs, 37
  supply chain management, 34
Commercialization of protocol, as monetization
    strategy, 139
Communication
  business network governance and, 115
  privacy of, 62

Competitive advantage, blockchain driving
    growth, 14
Compliance, blockchain opportunities, 35
Confidentiality, governance mechanisms, 107
Consensus
  blockchain technical vehicles for, 52
  decentralized networks, 107
  effective use of blockchain and, 80
  as technological challenge, 46
  token evaluation model, 77
  verification and fairness in transactions, 23–24
Consortiums
  business models for permissioned blockchain,
    96–97
  data ownership structure, 113
  overview of, 98–99
  resource optimization, 112
  risk optimization, 112
  roles in, 127
  table summarizing, 102
Consumability, of blockchain, 54–55
Consumer products, blockchain opportunities, 33
Contracts, smart. *See* Smart contracts
Control. *See also* Governance
  effective use of blockchain and, 80
  enterprise blockchain infrastructure and, 81
Corda
  in HACERA Unbounded Registry, 165
  interoperability and, 46
  open source blockchain platforms, 15
Costs
  of implementing blockchain, 15–16
  reducing with blockchain use, 2
Counterfeiting
  immutability of blockchain and, 21–22
  preventing, 11–12
CRM (Customer-relationship management), 54
Cross-chain transactions, exchange
    mechanisms, 78
Crypto Anchor Verifier project, 12
Crypto assets
  asset token fungibility, 75–76
  governance mechanisms, 107
  tokens compared with. *See also*
    Cryptocurrency, 73
Crypto developers, project team roles, 130
Cryptocurrency
  blockchain compared with bitcoin, 1
  blockchain foundation of, 40
  blockchain validation and, 23
  defined, 70

stable coins, 72

tokens compared with, 73

Cryptography

blockchain protocols, 51

challenges of adopting enterprise
blockchain, 50

Customer-relationship management (CRM), 54

Cybercurrency. *See also* Cryptocurrency, 52

Cybersecurity

identifying and preventing vulnerabilities, 22

quantum computing, 172–173

D

Data

clinical trials management, 32–33

eliminating breaches, 10–11

identifying and preventing security
vulnerabilities, 22

network membership governance and, 113

security of personal data, 168

Decentralization

consensus and, 107

distributed maintenance, 111

distributed organizational structure, 26–27

of ecosystem, 28–29

effective use of blockchain and, 80–81

intraprise synergy and, 133

organizational structure, 125

permissioned blockchain (public) and, 60

security benefits of blockchain, 23

Decentralized exchanges (DEXes), 78

Decision-making, consensus vehicles, 52

Deployment strategy, technology infrastructure
governance and, 112

Design

of blockchain network, 15

devising business blueprint, 90–91

devising technology blueprint, 91–92

separating business domain from supporting
technology, 63–65

token evaluation model, 76–77

Development team

dedicated blockchain development team, 15

project team roles, 130–132

DEXes (Decentralized exchanges), 78

Digital assets. *See* Tokenization

Digital fiat, 66–67

Digital identity

blockchain opportunities, 30

elements for enterprise blockchain
maturity, 66–67

Digitization. *See also* Tokenization

permissionless blockchain and, 70

token revolution and, 68

token value models in the instance economy, 74

Dispute resolution, membership governance
and, 113

Disruptive elements/technologies

consensus, 23–24

examples, 94

immutability, 21–22

mitigation of, 95

overview of, 20

security, 22–23

smart contracts, 24–25

transparency, 21

Distributed organizational structures. *See also*
Decentralization, 26–27

Distributed (shared) ledger, blockchain technical
building blocks, 51

Dream large and act incrementally, 6–7

E

Economic value, token evaluation model, 76–77

Economies of scale, business network governance
and, 115

Economy

blockchain economy, 164–167

instance economy, 73–74

peer-to-peer. *See* Peer-to-peer (P2P)

transaction-based, 61

Ecosystem

blockchain addressing key aspects of
transaction-based economy, 61

business ecosystem, 96–97, 99–100, 103

decentralized, 28–29

minimal viable. *See* Minimal viable
ecosystem (MVE)

Electronic data capture (EDC), 32

End-to-end supports, blockchain challenges, 47

Enterprise blockchain

applications, 56

attributes, 3–4

challenges of adopting, 49–50

elements required for maturity, 66–67

founders, 127

IBM Block chain free tiers, 16

illustration of, 57

members, 127

operators, 128

platform, 63

roles, 126

types of business networks and corresponding blockchain applications, 81–82

users, 128

Enterprise blockchain adoption

devising business blueprint, 90–91

devising technology blueprint, 91–92

ensuring integration with existing systems, 92

identifying appropriate use case, 89–90

overview of, 87–88

steps in, 88–89

Enterprise systems

business model analyzing impact of use case on, 89

integration of, 62

Entertainment, blockchain opportunities, 35–36

Escherichia coli (E. coli), reducing foodborne illness, 9–10

Ethereum

in HACERA Unbounded Registry, 165–166

interoperability and, 46

open source blockchain platforms, 15

The Event Ticketing solution, 6

eWallet

example of blockchain trailblazers, 6

mobility services, 38

Exchange conditions, business network governance and, 116

Exchange mechanisms

assets, 78–79

monetization and, 139

Extensibility, of blockchain network, 83–84

F

Facebook, 124

Fault-tolerance, 4

FDA (Food and Drug Administration), 4–5

Federated blockchain, 59

Finance

blockchain opportunities in financial markets, 29

building financial models, 141–143

trade finance benefits of blockchain, 29–30

Food and Drug Administration (FDA), 4–5

Food industry

benefits of blockchain to food industry, 4–5

reducing foodborne illness, 9–10

supply chain management, 34

The Foreign Currency Exchange, 5

Founders

blockchain organizational roles, 127

Build-Own-Operate. See Build-Own-Operate (BOO)

Build-Own-Operate-Transfer. See Build-Own-Operate-Transfer (BOOT)

Fraud

blockchain opportunities, 35

eliminating data breaches, 10–11

immutability of blockchain and, 21

Fungibility

asset exchange mechanisms and, 78–79

of asset tokens, 75–76

defined, 76

Future of blockchain

artificial intelligence (AI), 167–168

blockchain economy, 164–167

data security, 168

Internet of Things (IoT), 170–171

opportunities and challenges, 173–176

overview of, 163–164

quantum computing, 171–173

references, 180–181

summary, 176–180

transparency of AI decision making, 169–170

trusted AI models, 169

G

General Data Protection Regulation (GDPR)

accountability with, 3

transparency of AI decision making, 169–170

Goals, Specific, Measurable, Achievable, Results-focused, and Time-bound, 42

Google, 124

Governance

blockchain challenges, 43–44

of blockchain network, 15

business network governance, 114–117, 119

developing structure for blockchain networks, 105–109

effective use of blockchain and, 80

enterprise blockchain infrastructure and, 81

enterprise blockchain maturity and, 67

monetization strategy and, 147

network infrastructure governance, 120–121

network membership governance, 112–114, 120

risk modeling, 158–159

SCTrustNet governance structure, 118

structure and landscape, 109–110

summary, 121

technology infrastructure governance, 110–112

total is greater than sum of the parts and, 8

Governance, Risk, and Compliance (GRC)

business valuation techniques, 144

financial modeling and, 141–142

risk modeling, 158

technology infrastructure governance, 110, 112
Government
asset registration, 35
blockchain opportunities, 34–35
GRC. *See* Governance, Risk, and Compliance (GRC)
Groups, managing group benefits, 31–32
Growth
blockchain providing competitive advantage, 14
blockchain providing opportunities for, 2
monetization strategy and, 147–148

H

HACERA Unbounded Registry, 165
Health Insurance Portability and Accountability Act (HIPAA), 3
Healthcare
clinical trials management, 32–33
patient records management, 32
quality of care, 32
HIPAA (Health Insurance Portability and Accountability Act), 3
Hudson Quantum Initiative, 172–173
Hybrid blockchain
organizational structures, 125–126
types of blockchain, 59
Hyperledger
in HACERA Unbounded Registry, 165–166
interoperability and, 46
open source blockchain platforms, 15
scalability of blockchain solutions, 45

I

IACCM (International Association for Contract and Commercial Management), 24
IBM
joining HACERA Unbounded Registry, 165
supply chain management, 34
IBM Blockchain
China UnionPay loyalty program, 37
digital identity verification, 30
free tiers for implementing enterprise blockchain, 16
group benefits management, 31–32
reducing complexity of commercial transactions, 33
risk coverage in insurance industry, 31
IBM Food Trust Network
reducing foodborne illness, 9
supply chain management, 34
IBM Research Lab, 12

ICOs. *See* Initial coin offerings (ICOs)
Identity
digital verification, 30
eliminating identity theft, 10–11
The Identity Verification (Verified.me), 5, 10–11
IDs, eliminating data breaches, 10–11
Immutability, of blockchain technology, 21–22
Incentives. *See* Motivation
Industries
blockchain use cases, 68–69
business modeling and, 90
enterprise blockchain infrastructure and, 81–82
Information Technology Infrastructure Library (ITIL), 110
Infrastructure. *See also* Business structure; Organizational structure
identifying for team building, 129
network infrastructure governance, 120–121
separating business domain from supporting technology, 63–65
technology infrastructure governance, 110–112
token evaluation model, 77
Initial coin offerings (ICOs)
disruptive technologies, 94–95
example of new business design, 68
examples of distributed ecosystems, 28
fundraising tools, 138
Initiatives, blockchain types, 139–140
Instance economy, token value models in, 74
Insurance, blockchain opportunities, 30–31
Integration
blockchain with existing systems, 54, 82, 92
challenges of blockchain technologies, 47
high-level technology issues, 62
Internal rate of return (IRR)
business valuation techniques, 144
overview of, 151
valuation models for blockchain network, 150
International Association for Contract and Commercial Management (IACCM), 24
International Organization for Standardization (ISO), 50
The Internet of Loyalty, 6
Internet of Things (IoT), 170–171
Interoperability, blockchain challenges, 46–47
Intraprise synergy, 123, 132–133
Investment, examples of distributed ecosystems, 29
Investment rubric
business valuation, 146–147
governance and risk and, 147
growth and scale and, 147–148